Stories I Never Told Grandma

Eclectic short writings for the students of life.

Rich Kendall

DEDICATED TO PEWTER S. MANDEL

To Ronni,
Young at heart regardless of the years that pass.
With affection,
Rich Kendall

Cover Design and Composition by
Joni Tantillo/D&J Associates

ISBN: 978-0-9835776-4-5

Also by Rich Kendall:

The Road to Elmira, Volume 1

Contact Rich Kendall: highwaykendall@gmail.com

PREFACE

When I walked through the doors of Jane Roberts' apartment On January 4, 1972, a journey began that in one way or another we will all take. It is a journey through ourselves, and while the streets have no names, and the places we pass along the way have no addresses, the reality of where we have been cannot be denied.

RICH KENDALL
January, 2013

"Today is tomorrow, and present is past.
Nothing exists and everything will last.
There is no beginning, there was no end.
No depth to fall, no height to ascend.
There is only this moment, this flicker of light
That illuminates nothing, but oh! So bright!
For we are the spark that flutters in space,
Consuming an eternity of a moment's grace.
For today is tomorrow and present and past.
Nothing exists and everything will last."

Jane Roberts

CONTENTS

First Contact

Dear Jane and Rob,
I live in New York City, am twenty years old, and
my name is Richard Nissenbaum. I am studying and living
philosophy so as to bring into actuality the infinity of all
that I am. I have studied and continue to study books
by Carl Jung; such as Mysterium Coniunctionis, Aion, Psychology
and Alchemy, as well as books by many who far
exceeded the knowledge and understanding of Jung.
I would like to know if it would be
possible to visit you for even an hour or two to
read some of the other Seth material you have, and
of course if possible, attend a session. The access to
some of the knowledge in your unprinted material alone
would satisfy me greatly. If neither is possible, I
would appreciate it if you could find the time to
at least send me a postcard, telling me when to
expect the next book. Your respectful initiate:

Richard Nissenbaum
150-20-71 AVE
Kew Garden Hills,
N.Y.C. N.Y.

This is the letter I wrote Jane in the summer of 1971, asking if one day I could attend one of her classes. In rereading the letter today, I cringe at my closing remark of "Your respectful initiate." Yet it serves as a reference point, shedding light on the state of my consciousness and my beliefs at the time.

Each step we take on our journey is valid in and of itself, though at a later date such steps might seem foolish or embarrassing when viewed from the vantage point of our present psyche.

INTERVIEWS

Interview With A Limiting Belief

RK: First, I'd like to thank you for joining us today. I know your privacy is very important to you.

LB: *Yes. I've always felt that a low profile is the best way to go.*

RK: Now why is that? Do you think being too visible will expose you to danger?

LB: *Since I'm your limiting belief, maybe you should answer that question.*

RK: There's no need to get snippy about it.

LB: *You're right. It's just that lately I've been feeling that you really don't want me around anymore.*

RK: Well, I... If you really want to know the truth, I've been trying to break up with you for years, but haven't been able to find the courage until now.

LB: *Are you saying you're breaking up with me? Right now? In front of everyone? What about all we've been through together?*

RK: Yes, we have been through a lot together, but that isn't a good enough reason to stay together.

LB: *But where will I go? I've spent my entire life living inside of your psyche. It's the only home I've known.*

RK: I know it's upsetting right now, but there are plenty of other psyches that would be willing to take you in. Just be open to that possibility and I'm sure you'll meet someone else.

LB: *But NOT BEING OPEN defines who I am. I don't know if I can change after all these years.*

RK: If I can change, you can change.

LB: *I hope I didn't cause you too much trouble. I mean we did have some good times.*

RK: I don't know how good they were, but they served a purpose.

LB: *Just answer me this, I need to know: Have you met someone else? Please be honest. You owe me that.*

RK: The truth is I have met someone else. She believes that being visible and out in the world is not only good for the mind and body but also is quite safe. Overall I enjoy my life much more than I did when you and I were together.

LB: *I thought you liked being with me. After all, it was your choice whether to stay with me or not. It's not like I forced you to be with me.*

RK: That's true. You never forced me to stay with you. I did so out of my own free will.

LB: *(Starts to cry) But I gave you the best years of my life. If you weren't really happy why didn't you break up with me years ago?*

RK: I've wondered that same thing myself. I think a big part of it was that I didn't believe I had the right to be happy. I also believed it was important to suffer, and that suffering was good for the soul. But when that belief started to change, I ended up breaking up with a number of other beliefs as well.

LB: *You mean there have been others besides me?*

RK: C'mon. You knew that. You just liked to make believe you were the only one. It made you feel more important. And you *were* important. Each of my beliefs is important. Look, we had a pretty good run and there's no reason we have to part in anger. We can still be friends.

LB: *Does that mean I can visit at times?*

RK: You can visit, but you can't stay over.

LB: *Will you at least help me pack?*

RK: I'll help, but with all the baggage you're carrying around we need to get started right away. Just yesterday I came across a whole bunch of subsidiary beliefs that had been sitting in the bottom of the closet that I had completely forgotten about.

LB: *One last thing: You know I never intended to hurt you.*

RK: I realize that, but you know what they say about the road to hell being paved with good intentions.

LB: *Are you saying it's been hell living with me?*

RK: Let's just focus on the business at hand. There will be plenty of time later on to speculate about all we've been through. (opens closet door and starts to sort through stuff and sees the following belief written on a piece of paper): People will take advantage of you if you give them half a chance. Is this one yours or mine?

LB: *I think it's mine.*

RK: I can see this is going to be a long afternoon. Let's break for lunch. There's a small café up the street that makes these great burgers and also has the best fried chicken I've ever tasted.

LB: *Don't you know that fried foods aren't good for you?*

RK: You know what, maybe we should just continue packing and I'll grab lunch later.

LB: *That's fine. Wow, look at this stack of old beliefs I just found hidden in the corner. Between the both of us we really did accumulate a lot.*

RK: We sure did. We sure did.

Interview of Richard Kendall by Ursula Lang

Where do you think you would be today without Seth?

I assume when you ask "where" you are not referring to a geographical area but to an inner psychological state. Sitting on a balcony in the French Riviera overlooking the Mediterranean will bring little joy if one's psyche is in turmoil. So to the point of your question, if I had never been exposed to the ideas embodied in the Seth material, there's a good chance that when I looked out at the world today, regardless of where I was physically situated, I'd see a planet filled with senseless suffering, endless greed, and horrendous injustices.

But thankfully, because of the concepts embodied in the Seth material, I can find order and meaning in what seems to be chaos, and glimpse an inner cooperation between all species that renders labels such as victim and perpetrator as meaningless.

What influences or effects of the Seth Material do you see in the mass event Framework One world today?

I don't keep up much with world events, but in the creative arts, concepts that might have been considered very far out when Jane began speaking for Seth in 1963 are appearing with increasing frequency today. For example, I became hooked on the television series *Lost,* which played to millions of people. Lately the show has been exploring the idea of alternate realities, or parallel existences.

In the realm of movies I recently saw *Sliding Doors,* which tackles the subject of probable realities and does an excellent job in the process. And in the movie *Heaven Can Wait* with Warren Beatty, reincarnation is a major theme, and no doubt there are many other examples that one could cite.

Tell us about Jane and Rob, the persons you knew outside of class.

To say I was good friends with Jane and Rob in the way that friends often visit with each other or regularly speak on the phone would not be true.

But it would be true to say that their door was always open to me and that if I needed help they would be there for me.

Outside of a class setting Jane was very at ease with people. Her conversation could range over a variety of subjects, yet wherever the conversation went she was always trying to find the inner meanings that lay beneath the details. She was like a psychic detective always on the lookout for clues to help solve the mysteries of how reality creation operated. She also had a great and at times wicked sense of humor.

Rob on the other hand had a very different temperament. He was more of a loner and more subdued by nature. I think he was most comfortable when in his studio painting. He could be quite serious at times. I remember once, having lost track of the time, I arrived at class an hour early. Rob came out into the living room and when he saw me sitting there, he stared at me with a very stern expression. He then conveyed his displeasure at my having arrived so early. I promptly left and felt like a kid who had just walked out of the principal's office after being chastised for some inappropriate behavior during class.

But Rob's integrity and devotion to the Seth material, as well as his devotion to Jane, demonstrate the kind of individual he was. Rob played an essential role in the development and dissemination of the Seth material. His contributions should not be underestimated.

What do you think are they up to now?

I'm glad you used the word "think" because I tend to doubt that anyone can really specifically know what others are up to once they "pass over." Furthermore, I also tend to doubt that the answer could adequately be expressed in words. But I do wonder at times if Jane or Rob are aware of current developments pertaining to the Seth material, and whether they ever look in on former students as well.

My feeling is that any communication is likely to take place in the dream state and while I don't dream of Jane often she does appear in my dreams every now and then. What would be interesting to me would be to know if any of their ideas about reality as presented in their books have changed since they passed, and if so, in what ways.

Are you still in contact with the members of Jane's ESP class?

Some of those folks I am in touch with and others I haven't spoken to in a very long time. Some I have just lost track of. But since class has ended I have developed some very fulfilling friendships with people who never went to class but who have read the Seth books and try to incorporate the ideas into their daily living.

Do you think you are a different person (personality) now than at the time of the classes?

I think personality constantly changes and we are never exactly the same person from one day to the next. But one of the lasting changes within myself that I attribute directly to the Seth material is that I have become more willing to allow my vulnerability to show, and hence are less defensive in my interactions with others.

What are you doing now in the present, in the year 2010?

I have a number of things I am involved with right now. One of them is working with a company in Los Angeles that owns the movie rights to Jane's novel *The Education of Oversoul 7*, for which I am trying to find investors. I am also busy writing my own book entitled, *The Road To Elmira*. And I also enjoy composing songs on my guitar.

Tell us please about your book.

The Road To Elmira is a work in progress where I take various comments Seth made to me during the years I attended Jane's classes, and explore them in terms of how they affected my life at the time, and how they continue to affect my life today.

How do you see the future of the Seth material?

Like my book, I think the future of the Seth material is also a work in progress, and with probabilities always being in play, nothing is predetermined. I also think the consciousness of many people has already been changed by Seth's ideas, and that the material continues to circulate through the mass psyche in various ways.

And if one day a new and better paradigm is established for mankind to live by, I believe the Seth material will have played a significant role in that change. On a personal level I continue to work with the seeds that were planted in my psyche those many years ago, and no doubt I will be doing so until the end of my life.

A CHIP OFF THE OLD BLOCK

The Morris Nissenbaum Coincidence

In 1987, my father (Morris Nissenbaum) had a coincidence that made quite an impression upon him. I asked him to write it up for inclusion in a magazine called "Coordinate Point" that my friend Jan Sweeney was publishing at the time. Here is what he wrote.

1

Dear Jan:

As promised, the story of my dental problem:

On Friday evening, August 1, as I was having dinner, a fixed bridge consisting of three teeth in the upper part of my mouth, directly in front, broke off leaving me with an unsightly gap when I spoke or smiled.

Needless to say, I immediately got on the phone and called my dentist at his office but there was no answer and so I was forced to wait until Saturday morning when I tried him again but still no answer. I spent the better part of Saturday morning calling him, trying to get his home number with no success and finally at about 1:00PM I gave up and resigned myself to the fact that I would have to wait until Monday to contact him.

Unfortunately, my wife and I had scheduled a flight to the Bahamas this Saturday afternoon, so with much reluctance and a resolve to keep my mouth closed for the weekend, we departed for Miami Airport. Once in the airport, we routinely went through the security check, my wife placing her bag on the track and picking it up on the other side of the scanner. As she did so, she noticed off the Counter a folded brochure that said in bold print "FLY FREE." Curious, she picked it up and as we were strolling along to our gate, she opened it and inside was an application form in small print. Not

2

having her glasses handy, she passed it over to me to read. I glanced at it and there was only one line that had been filled out.

Where it said "name" on the top line was written Wm. Paul DeMirza, the full name of my dentist whom I had been trying to contact all morning. I was stunned, could not believe my eyes. We both dashed to the Delta gate thinking he might still be there, but the plane had just finished boarding.

When I saw my dentist the following week, and showed him the brochure, it was indeed his writing. He had taken a brochure, started to fill it out, changed his mind, and left it on the counter. He had traveled to Montreal that day to attend a dental conference and you can imagine he was as astounded as I was.

I still find it hard to believe that of the many thousands of people passing through Miami Airport that day, Dr. DeMirza left what seemed to be a message advising me that he was out of town.

Morris Nissenbaum
15018 S.W. 127 Circle Place N.
Miami, FL

TEMPORARY IDENTIFICATION CARD
DELTA FREQUENT FLYER
AUTOMATED MILEAGE PROGRAM

DELTA FREQUENT FLYER AUTOMATED MILEAGE PROGRAM
APPLICATION
(Please print or type – Each individual must enroll separately)

Name: Wm PAUL DeMIRZA
(First) (MI) (Last)
Mailing Address: ☐ home ☐ business
(Number) (Street) (Suite #)
(City) (State) (Zip)
Company
Business Phone (Area) (Number)
Home Phone (Area) (Number)

If you are already enrolled in Delta's Frequent Flyer or Crown Room Programs, it will not be necessary to submit another application. Do not use application for address changes.

DELTA FREQUENT FLYER
AUTOMATED MILEAGE PROGRAM

DELTA FREQUENT FLYER AWARDS
DOMESTIC BONUS TRAVEL AWARDS** (DELTA/AIR CANADA)

Revenge of the Gumballs

I was walking around Greenwich Village one evening, killing some time before going to meet a friend, when I noticed this gumball machine on the sidewalk in front of a sweet shop. Gumballs are those large, round, colored pieces of gum that kids love to test their teeth on, often to a parent's dismay. But all it takes is a quarter and a turn of the handle, and like some small planet thrown out of its orbit, we watch with delight as the orb descends to earth, crashing against the metal lid at the bottom of the machine. For a moment we become the gumball's savior as we lift back the lid and let the gumball fall safely into our hands. But a false Messiah we are indeed. For rather than becoming its savior, we promptly devour it as it collapses beneath the crushing force of our teeth.

Reduced to a mere shell of its former self, the gumball usually ends up sprawled on some sidewalk, left to suffer the ignominious fate of being stepped upon by endless anonymous feet, until some rainstorm washes it down a nearby sewer. Not a great ending for what might have been a promising future.

As I stood there staring at the machine, I decided what the hell, reached into my pocket, and pulled out a quarter. Just as I was about to insert the quarter into the slot I suddenly felt a clear impulse NOT to follow through with this. I remember thinking I could always use the quarter at the Laundromat, so why waste it on a gumball. I then thought how stupid that was, to worry about spending a quarter. So I put the money in the slot, turned the handle, and watched in triumph as the gumball made its way down the chute and shortly thereafter into my mouth.

Although the gumball was a lot harder than gumballs I had encountered in the past, as I heard it crack I felt a sense of pride that even though I was not so young anymore, my teeth were still strong enough to crush a gumball,. There was just one minor detail to contend with: three of those teeth which were part of a bridge that had been affixed in my mouth were no longer in my mouth—but sitting within the wad of gum I now held in my hand.

Was this some form of poetic justice, the gumball's revenge for how shabbily its species has been treated over the years? Whatever it was, there wasn't much I could do about it at the moment. So I put the part of my mouth that was no longer in my mouth into my shirt pocket and continued on my journey to hook up with a friend.

One of the first questions that inevitably arises in any discussion about impulses is how do we differentiate between what I'll call true impulses, which when followed enrich our lives, and impulses that will bring unpleasant ramifications. I believe there is a part of us that always knows the difference. Whether we allow that knowledge to come to the surface, or listen to it when it does, is another story. But I believe the knowledge is always there, as it was plainly there in my gumball experience. I remember the quite conscious decision to ignore a clear impulse telling me NOT to put that quarter in the slot. In this case, the result of my not listening was manifested almost instantaneously.

True impulses are direct communications from our inner self, private messengers carrying the results of probability computations that would dwarf the capabilities of the most sophisticated computers. The mechanics of those inner computations need not concern the conscious mind, nor would it be able hold them. But the decision to heed these messages can save us all kinds of grief, not to mention exorbitant dental bills.

So what I learned that day can be condensed as follows:
Gumballs and impulses are not things to be trifled with, no matter how old you are ...or how young you wish you were.

Sister's Letter

When I first started attending Jane Roberts' classes, my parents were not very happy about it. Having come from a traditional Jewish background, they simply had no reference for what I was becoming involved with. It also didn't help that I made no attempt to explain or share with them what this "Seth stuff" was all about.

One night while I was at my parents' apartment, I was sitting in the kitchen with a friend of mine and playing a tape recording I had made of Jane singing Sumari. It was about 2:00am and I didn't realize that the volume had been turned up far more than it should have been for that time of night. The recording woke up my father, and he stormed into the kitchen and let loose a rant about how I was becoming involved with all this crazy, dangerous stuff. I shut off the tape recorder and didn't say anything in response. I didn't feel there was anything I could say that would change his opinion of what I was involved in, or for that matter, his opinion of me. He then stormed back into his bedroom.

A few years later my sister remarried and she and her husband moved down to Florida to start a new life. Uncharacteristically for my parents, without having a job or a place to live, they followed suit. They lived with my sister and her new husband for about eight months, found work, moved into their own apartment, and never looked back. Following that impulse to go to Florida was one of the best decisions they had ever made, as they spent many happy years in the sunshine state.

As for me, I chose to stay in New York; (well, actually, I wasn't invited to join them) but I wouldn't have gone in any event. Over the years, contact with my folks was sparse, but one day I received a note from my sister regarding my father. He had gone to a library book sale and on impulse bought a copy of the book, *The Seth Material*. I never asked him what he thought about the book's contents, but the very fact that he went out and bought a copy of that book spoke volumes in and of itself.

What follows is the excerpt from the note I received from my sister those many years ago.

Dear Richard, 12/10/93

Happy Hanukkah and best wishes for a sparkling New Year.

Daddy went to the library book sale and bought a Seth book, which he is reading. Last night, he actually called to ask if I had a ouija board

OTHER FACES

Mayan Connection

In 1995, I received a card from Angela Murphy, a friend and fellow Seth reader who I hadn't heard from in a number of years. In the card she wrote a note speaking of a possible life I may have lived as a Mayan woman. Many years earlier, unbeknownst to Angela, friend and compatriot Susan Watkins told me of a vision she had of me as a Mayan woman.

As related to me by Susan M. Watkins sometime around 1980:

I saw you one day as a Mayan woman planting crops when a swarm of yellow jackets came up from behind and attacked you. You ended up dying from the attack.

Angela's comment and Sue's vision, both produced independently of each other, sure did make me wonder. This is the card along with Angela's note.

Tue March 7 '95

Hi R.K.
I don't know why, but I saw this card and thought of you. Have you ever had any sensation of being part of the Mayan culture? I have.

Indian Dream

One night during class, Jane Roberts looked at me and unrelated to anything that was happening in class at the moment, said, "Rich, you were an Indian." That's all she said and then continued on with class. I didn't ask her anything more about her statement but had often felt strong connections with American Indians at various times in my life. Some years later, I had this very vivid dream I want to share with you.

In the dream I was an American Indian, sitting upon a horse, and looking out upon a large field. Then seemingly out of nowhere, another Indian came riding up swiftly behind me, and before I had a chance to react, he struck me squarely on the head with his tomahawk. I fell off my horse and my body started rolling on the ground though I was not in any pain.

In the next instant I found myself sitting up in the dream, and though my eyes were closed (in the dream) a picture began to form within my mind. The picture was of a beautiful blue nighttime sky, with the moon shining in the background. I then opened my eyes (in the dream) and when I did so I saw and felt a woman's arms and hands reaching across my body from behind. There was an incredible sense of healing energy which began to emanate from the softness and warmth of her hands, and strong feelings of peace began to fill my entire body. I instinctively knew I wasn't supposed to look behind me to see her image, and I didn't feel the need or desire to do so.

Still dreaming, I wondered if I was dead, and had the impulse to open my eyes (in this reality) but was a bit concerned that when I did I would find out that I really had died. I was also resistant to opening my eyes because I didn't want to lose the feelings of tranquility I was experiencing in the dream.

I then opened my eyes (in this reality) and the feelings of peace I had experienced in the dream carried over for a short time into this reality. Also, as I felt the folds of the blanket that lay by my side in the bed, they felt exactly like the woman's arms and hands in the dream. This sensation lasted only a few seconds after which I fully awoke, and the folds of the blanket once more became simply the folds of a blanket.

One last thing I remember is that someone was reciting a poem of some

Marguerite de Valois

On March 28, 1972, while sitting in the living room of Jane Roberts, Seth turned to me and said the following:

"Now, the small but brilliant sardonic part of you was, and in other terms still is, a very brilliant courtesan in sixteenth century France who sat with the philosophers and thought they did not know what they were talking about, and thought, 'they have not the slightest idea in their heads, and yet they look at me and think I am beautiful and silly when I can think rings around them;' and so you did, and in other terms, so you still do. This woman had much energy and still possesses it."

I certainly found Seth's words intriguing, but at the time they didn't evoke any strong feelings within me, and I wasn't inclined to start searching through French history books to try to figure out who this mysterious and nameless woman might have been. In December of that year, nine months after Seth had given me this information, I became curious about the Belgian artist, René Magritte, after attending an art exhibit in New York City which featured his paintings. I decided to go to the public library to learn more about Magritte's life.

While at the library, I picked up the encyclopedia (this was pre-Google days) and began to read about Magritte. Suddenly, on the facing page, the name Marguerite de Valois jumped up at me. There were only a few lines written about her, but one of them stated that she was a well-known courtesan in sixteenth century France. This comment immediately brought to mind the information Seth had given me earlier in the year. The following week I went back to the library to see what I could find out about this Marguerite de Valois character.

To my surprise there were numerous listings which contained her name, but what really sent a jolt to my psyche was the following reference: Secret and Historic Memoirs of the Courts Of France, written by Marguerite De Valois. I filled out the slip the librarian needed to retrieve the book, and when the book arrived, I read a few pages, and decided I would ask Seth about this woman at next week's class. So the following week I asked Seth if he cared to say anything about a Margaret de Valois. He looked at me with what seemed like an odd expression and said:

"Not now, I do not. But I appreciate the reason for the question."

Later, during that same class, he looked at me and said: "Marguerite," correcting my earlier mispronunciation when I had said Margaret. Despite the brevity of Seth's response, I now felt something was up, and went back to the library to begin my research in earnest.

Marguerite of Valois in 1555 attributed to François Clouet

Marguerite de Valois as a young girl

Over the next few months I spent many hours researching Marguerite's life, and during this time, events in my life began to mirror events in her life that I would be currently reading about. For example, one day I was reading about a time in Marguerite's life when the court was set up in the city of Navarre. As I left the library that day and was walking around Manhattan, I passed a hotel called Hotel Navarre. In all my years of wandering the city I had never come across this hotel prior to that day.

Another incident occurred when I was reading about one of Marguerite's first love affairs. She was in love with a well-known military leader named the Duke d' Guise, and it was fully expected they would marry. One day, to Marguerite's great surprise, and with no attempt to soften the news, the Duke informed her he had chosen another to marry him and his proposal had been accepted. Shortly thereafter, I called a woman I was growing increasingly fond of, and to my great surprise, and with no attempt to soften the news, she informed me that a friend of ours had asked her to marry him and that she had accepted his proposal.

As I continued my research I not only found connections between events in Marguerite's life and my own, but parallels in personality characteristics. (See Chapter 8 of my book, *The Road To Elmira, Volume 1,* for more details.)

I also began to get feelings about people I knew now, and who they might have been during the time that Marguerite lived. For example, I had the distinct feeling that my friend Ricky was this well-known soldier named Duke d' Guise, of whom I spoke of earlier. The more I read about the Duke d' Guise, the more I began to see connections between Ricky and the Duke's life and personality. One day when going through some old pictures, I found one of Ricky that shows a remarkable similarity to a picture I have of the Duke.

On September 29, 1979, I went to what turned out to be the last official Seth class Jane ever held. I felt I had to get some answers from Seth regarding the research I had done. After some preliminary comments, Seth finally corroborated the fact that Marguerite de Valois was the woman he was referring to years earlier when he gave me that reincarnational information. He also verified that Ricky was indeed the Duke d' Guise as I had surmised.

Classes ended, and as the years went by I spent little time thinking about Marguerite de Valois or the Duke d' Guise, or sixteenth century France in general. Then in 1990, eleven years after that last Seth class, a friend and I spent a week in Bolton Landing, a small town near Lake George, which is a popular vacation spot in upstate New York.

While vacationing there, we picked up a tourist brochure from one of the local shops, and one of the places mentioned in the brochure was The *Madame Sembrich Museum*. I'm not much of a museum person, but after some prodding by my friend I agreed to go. Neither of us had any idea who this Madame Sembrich was, but later learned that she was a famous opera singer in the late nineteenth and early twentieth century. Originally from Poland, she came to the United States in 1883, and performed at The Metropolitan Opera House in New York City more than four hundred times.

The museum in Bolton Landing was her former studio where Madame Sembrich had rehearsed and taught young vocalists, and it contained various memorabilia from her career. Part of the memorabilia included original costumes she wore from various operas she had appeared in. Alongside each costume there was a card listing the name of the opera and the character that Madame Sembrich had played.

All of a sudden, one of the cards caught my eye. It had the word Huguenots written upon it. The Huguenots were the French Protestants in sixteenth century France and they figured prominently in the research I had done so many years earlier. The card said that this particular gown was worn by Madame Sembrich in the opera Les Huguenots, during her portrayal of... Marguerite De Valois!

A little-known opera about Marguerite De Valois was one thing, but it was quite another when Sue Watkins (author of *Conversations*

With Seth) called me in 1994 to tell me of a review she had just read of a movie entitled Queen Margot, based on the life of Marguerite De Valois. I grabbed a newspaper and checked the movie section to see where it might be playing. What a "coincidence": it was showing right up the block from where I worked.

I wondered about all these synchronicities. Were they being created by Marguerite to make sure I didn't forget about her, or was I the one responsible for their creation. Perhaps we were sending messages to each other; clues for each of us to follow in our separate yet related journeys. Whatever the answers might be, there always seemed to be just one more event waiting in the wings to show itself, so that our connection would never be forgotten.

In May of 2012, a friend of mine from The Netherlands, named Deborah, came to Connecticut to attend a wedding. We got together one evening and had a fun time discussing the Seth material. During the evening, Marguerite De Valois kept coming to mind. I felt a strong impulse to show Deborah pictures I had of Marguerite, and with my apartment being only a short distance from where Deborah was staying, I went home, put the pictures in a folder, and proceeded to share them with her.

The next day, Deborah was planning to take the train into New York City where there were a number of places she wanted to visit. One of those places was the Frick Museum, where there was a Renoir exhibit she wanted to see. I asked if I could join her and she said yes. As I walked into the room containing the Renoir paintings, the very first picture I looked at really bothered me, though I had no idea why. I had such a negative reaction to it that I decided I wouldn't read the plaque below the picture, which gave background information about the painting, and which I would normally always be curious to read.

The room contained only nine pictures by Renoir, and after viewing all of them except that first one to which I had the negative reaction to, I decided before we left I might as well review that one as well. The title by the way was Madame Henriot "en travesti" (The Page). Below is the information that accompanied the painting.

"Renoir's eighteen-year-old model, Marie-Henriette Grossin – an actress who later adopted the stage name Madame Henriot – appears before a red velvet curtain, with a glimpse of the theater behind her. She is playing a boy's role, as we can see from her costume, and wears a long-sleeved doublet with buttons fastened tightly down the center, reminiscent of a troubadour. Eager to make his mark as a painter of theatrical celebrities, Renoir may have posed Henriot as the beautiful page Urbain, who serves Queen *Marguerite de Valois* in Les Huguenots, an immensely popular opera set in the sixteenth century. Henriot had no training as a singer and could never have appeared in this opera; she was performing supporting roles in one of Paris's minor theaters at the time."

After seeing the name Marguerite de Valois my consciousness just came to an abrupt stop. I've had this kind or reaction before when reality seems to turn sideways as certain kinds of data presents itself. When I regained my mental composure, I thought about the night before, and how I had felt Marguerite's presence and was so intent on showing Deborah pictures of Marguerite. My reaction to that Renoir painting made me wonder if I was picking up Marguerite's feelings regarding a page that had served her in sixteenth century France.

MARGUERITE DE VALOIS, QUEEN OF NAVARRE

Queen Marguerite at the time of marriage to King Henry III of Navarre

There are connections and correspondences between selves that speak to each of us in a variety of ways. Sometimes they peek out at us from paintings; or come to us as images across a screen in a local movie house; or wait to catch our eye in a small museum we visit simply on impulse. However they make themselves known, they are always near, waving to us, calling our names, whistling tunes. But we usually just attribute the unknown sounds to the wind playing tricks on us. If it is just the wind, what miraculous breezes blow through the centuries, carrying strands of consciousness that weave in and out of our daily lives so seamlessly we often don't notice them. But each time we do notice them, the tapestry of our lives becomes that much richer.

JUMPING THE SYNAPSES

Breaking Hearts

What unwritten histories have we shared through the centuries? What memories lay hidden behind your eyes that my heart senses in odd moments of silence between us? I still feel the sting of broken promises made centuries ago in distant lands, as spellbound by the scent of your perfumed hair I found you in the arms of the emperor's nephew. Yet as surely as you broke my heart, I know there were times I broke yours as well. Wonder what the score is. Wonder whose turn it is now. I'm not certain but I'm pretty sure that it's my turn now.

Yes, I definitely think it's my turn now. I will plan it craftily. I shall slowly gain your trust and when all your defenses have come down I will launch a perfect arrow of deceit deep into your heart. And as you discover my unfaithfulness, how sweet the revenge will be. I will replay the scene in mind's eye over and over again. How peaceful I will sleep that night.

Would I have it in me to act in such a callous manner? Indeed I would. All I would have to do is remember that time in Santa Cruz when you seduced both father and son and boasted of it unashamedly while sharing my bed when you needed shelter.

Yes, I think it's my turn now. So I will be patient, and cautious, and not give the game away until the very end. A triumph of trickery will be mine. And despite all your prideful efforts, tears will stream down those beautiful rosy cheeks, carrying more pain than you would have imagined could arise from something as mundane as a faithless lover.

And next time it will be your turn. Or perhaps I could go twice in a row. No, that wouldn't be fair, and really mean. And neither of us would want to be like that, would we?

Sentimental Journey

There were flowers in the room, but they kept disappearing, and then appearing again, but no one minded.

Her smile once melted me, and I lay there in a shimmering pool of my own bliss, from which I actually had some difficulty emerging.

I once told her I didn't want to grow old without her, and she said I would do just fine. Her response made me angry because I wanted her to say the same; that she didn't want to grow old without me.

She once called me a thief– said that I had stolen her heart. But she forgave me. She always forgave me.

I remember telling her one day that I felt bad that I had gained so much weight, and knew that my youthful good looks had lost their edge. That night, she cooked me a pasta dinner with rich cream sauces, and for desert, made raspberry tarts sprinkled with bits of chocolate.

I was finishing a bowl of Cheerios and milk one September evening in 1999, when I felt the presence of another consciousness within my own. The words written above were silently spoken by that other consciousness, yet the emotions associated with those words resonated throughout my whole body as if they were mine. At the same time I knew such was not the case. I was stunned by what had occurred and wasn't sure what to make of it.

For some reason I thought of Stan Ulkowski, who had passed away in March of that same year. Stan, with long-time companion Lynda Dahl, started Seth Network International, a non-profit organization which published a magazine called Reality Change, which connected Seth readers from all over the world. Lynda and Stan also sponsored numerous Seth conferences, and overall they did a great job of leading people to explore Seth's ideas in new ways.

The same month that Stan had passed away I started a new job for a company situated in Brooklyn, New York. Having worked as a paralegal for the same law firm in Manhattan for over fifteen years, beginning a new job represented new beginnings on many levels.

It was now November and I was entitled to a week's vacation from work. I had been in a long-term relationship which recently ended, and as a result this was the first vacation I'd be taking by myself in many years. I wasn't sure where to go and decided to be playful and make a game of it.

The game would be that I would go online, open up a virtual map of the United States, and whatever cities "called out to me" is where I would visit. As I looked over the map I found myself drawn to a number of towns along the southern coast of California, between San Diego and Laguna Beach. So being true to the game, the southern coast of California it would be.

I decided to make Carlsbad, California my home base. I had never been to Carlsbad, or any of the cities south of Los Angeles, so I was looking forward to some new scenery and some new experiences.

About a week before I was scheduled to go on my vacation, I wrote a silly note to Lynda Dahl on the back of a postcard. It was one of many impulsive acts I had begun to follow as of late. In the note I told her how fondly I recalled that delicious seafood dinner we shared, and how spectacular the sunset had been as we sat by the pier. None of this happened in official time, or official terms, so I hesitated for a moment to send the note, but then decided what the hell.

I went up the block to drop it off at the nearby mailbox, and at that exact moment the postman was emptying the contents of the mailbox into his mailbag. I asked if I could put in one more and he said sure. And then I completely forgot about it.

It was now the eve of my departure for Carlsbad, and I was trying to do ten-thousand things at once. Just as I started to pack, the phone rang. It was my former landlady, who had recently moved from Brooklyn to New Jersey. She was usually not one to stay on the phone very long, but this night she was very talkative. I didn't want to be rude, so I waited until the conversation reached a natural end, said goodbye, and then continued to get ready for my trip.

I made it as far as the next room before the phone rang again. It was a friend from California whom I hadn't heard from in quite a while. She had no idea of my upcoming trip nor did I tell her about it. I wasn't really up for getting together with anyone and just wanted to be free to follow my spontaneous leanings without having any kind of a schedule. Again, I let the conversation take its natural course and hung up the phone, feeling confident that now I could finally begin making some real headway in preparing for my trip.

That lasted all of about thirty seconds as the phone rang once more. This time I answered it with obvious annoyance in my voice and for a moment, I didn't recognize who the caller was. "Come on, you know who this is," was the response on the other end, and I realized it was Lynda Dahl.

I had forgotten all about that silly note I had mailed to her earlier in the week, and that's what she was calling about. She was curious if the note related to a dream I recently had or if there was any particular story behind it. I told her it didn't have anything to do with a dream, and that I was just a silly guy who wrote silly notes.

We went on to talk of other things, and I told her I was leaving tomorrow for vacation. She naturally asked where I was intending to go, and when I told her the towns I would be visiting, she paused, and then informed me that she and Stan had lived in that exact area of southern California for many years. Although I continued to get ready for my trip, I couldn't help taking a few moments to think about the information Lynda had just shared with me. I began to wonder: Whose memory did that seafood dinner and spectacular sunset really belong to?

As I sat at the airport the next morning waiting to board my flight to San Diego, the song, "I Love You for Sentimental Reasons" kept running through my head. It was frustrating because I could only remember a few lines. The flight was uneventful, and while peacefully cruising above the clouds I remembered part of a dream I had the week before. In the dream I was standing on the steps of a building in Eugene, Oregon, and there was some decision I had to make involving the building. During the time Lynda and Stan were running Seth Network International they were living in Eugene, but I wasn't sure what the dream meant. The plane began its final descent, and though I purposefully hadn't made any arrangements as to how I would be getting from the airport in San Diego to my hotel in Carlsbad, I didn't feel concerned.

After deplaning and picking up my luggage, I asked someone who worked at the airport how I could get to Carlsbad. He told me there were shuttle vans right outside the terminal that took passengers up and down the coast. So I hopped on one of these vans, which was from a company called *Cloud Nine*, which ended up being an apt description.

As the van began to make its way up the coast toward Carlsbad, I unexpectedly started to experience intense feelings of ecstasy. The intensity of the emotions went far beyond the normal sense of relaxation or mellowness one might feel while being on vacation. These feelings accompanied me the entire way up the coast to Carlsbad.

Rich Kendall, Carlsbad California, 1999

As I checked into my hotel room the first thing I noticed was the refrigerator. It was the exact model I had back home in Brooklyn. It was the same size, same color, and the blue ice cube trays in the freezer were the same ones I had at home, which just yesterday I had contemplated throwing out. The only difference was that this refrigerator door opened from the right side while the one at home opened from the left. Not a momentous connection for sure, but something about it struck me. Two versions of a refrigerator to reflect two versions of a self? I had only been in Carlsbad for a short time but started to get the feeling that a probable self of mine had been living there for a lot longer than that.

After unpacking I went out to do a bit of local sightseeing, and walked along the ocean which was right across the street from where I was staying. Later that evening I dined at Angel's Burgers, thoroughly enjoying my avocado burger, fries, and large root beer soda. I walked back to the hotel, and as day one of my vacation in Carlsbad drew to a

Rich Kendall, Oceanside California, 1999

close, one question came to mind: What the hell am I doing here?

I woke up the next morning a little before 5:00AM without remembering even a snippet of a dream. I took a leisurely stroll by the water and thought about what to do for the day. One of the places I had felt compelled to visit was San Juan Capistrano, which is about thirty miles north of Carlsbad. The only thing I knew about San Juan Capistrano was that it was home to what was supposed to be the oldest mission in the United States.

I took the local bus to the transit center in Oceanside, where I transferred to an Amtrak train which stopped only a few blocks from the mission. As I entered the mission, a sense of serenity crept over me. And then, an odd feeling entered my consciousness—a sense of pride followed by the thought "I am glad the mission is still here." Once again, uncharacteristic feelings and thoughts rose to the surface.

The church bells from the mission began to ring and I actually shed a tear. It wasn't from sadness, but from a feeling of coming home, and part of me didn't want to leave. Where these feelings were coming from I didn't know.

I then went into the main chapel and found myself sitting alone in one of the pews. I heard chanting coming from one of the nearby rooms, and as I listened to the sounds, which were quite beautiful, I understood something that I couldn't adequately explain in words. I understood the yearning that people have to be comforted by someone or something outside of themselves.

I then glanced up and saw a huge bas-relief depicting Jesus hanging upon a cross. Large heavy nails were driven deep into his hands, and the blood, bright red and thick, was dripping down his wrists. The sculpture jolted me out of my reverie. I exited the chapel and spent some time walking among the gardens that surrounded the mission.

As I was leaving, I noticed a plaque on the outside wall that read in part "Vaya Con Dias—Go with God." Vaya Con Dias is one of the last lines spoken in the movie *The Magnificent Seven*, and I had always wondered what that phrase meant, though for some reason I never took the time to look it up. I recalled that when I first heard those words spoken in the movie, they evoked a strong emotional reaction within me; as did my visit to the Mission in San Juan Capistrano.

The next morning I was back at the transit center in Oceanside; this time to buy tickets for San Clemente, one of the towns that had "summoned me" when I was deciding where I would go on my vacation. When I got off the local bus at Oceanside, I saw a Greyhound Bus with the words "Los Angeles" written on it. I asked the driver if the bus stopped at San Clemente and he said yes, but he was just about to leave. He told me if I got a ticket right away he would wait. I ran to the ticket counter, bought a ticket, and off we went.

When the bus dropped me off in San Clemente I asked someone where the downtown area was. He told me to go to Del Mar and make a left. As I began to walk to Del Mar, the weather this particular day was without exaggeration the most perfect weather in memory I had ever experienced. I felt connected to the weather in a way that I had never felt before. It was as if my senses were in a heightened state of awareness from the moment I stepped into that van in San Diego.

As I continued walking I passed a shop that had a big sign above it which read: Sentimental Journey. Those words hinted at something that was happening to me during this trip that I couldn't as yet put my finger on.

When I reached the downtown area, I parked myself on a bench at the corner of Del Mar and South El Camino. Feeling like I was in a mild trance state, I took out a small notebook from my shirt pocket and wrote the following:

"I sit on a bench at the corner of Del Mar and South El Camino and mourn a relationship that never was and never will be. I struggle against this eventuality while knowing that there is nothing I can do about it.

"Images of Richard Nixon, (former President of the United States) now cross my mind. I remember that he had a home in San Clemente. I was no fan of Nixon yet I recall how badly I felt for him while watching his resignation speech on television, and how he just rambled on and on as he was fighting back tears.

"I see a man in a red convertible sports car drive by. He catches my attention because he looks remarkably like an older version of Stan Ulkowski. I begin to feel as if I'm tiptoeing around the edges of someone else's life, yet it seems to be my life as well. There is something here for me to understand; yet I know the understanding will not come with words.

"An elderly lady wearing what looks like a leopard skin hat slowly makes her way across the street. As I watch her cross it is as if each scene I look at is etched with a sharpness and clarity that goes beyond our usual way of perceiving reality. Suddenly I know my time in San Clemente is at an end.

"As I wait for the bus to take me back to Oceanside, I'm leaning on a mailbox at a busy intersection at the corner of Mendocino and South El Camino Real. A steady stream of traffic flows by. Part of me keeps expecting one of those cars at any moment to turn off the freeway, drive straight up to me, and as the car door opens, Stan Ulknowski and Lynda Dahl will tell me to get in. I feel like part of me has been standing at that intersection for centuries."

I woke up the next morning remembering parts of a dream involving Lynda Dahl. In the dream I was on a local bus, and Lynda was sitting next to me. She leans over and offers me her cheek in a gesture of friendship. I was supposed to place my cheek next to hers which I did, and then kissed her cheek. That's all I remembered.

After breakfast I got on the bus and headed down the coast with the intention of visiting the town of Del Mar. The ride down the coast was beautiful, but when we reached Del Mar, instead of getting off the bus I decided to continue going south to the last stop, which was called University Town Centre, near the University of California, San Diego. After just a few minutes I boarded the same bus back, and the driver, who was the same one who had driven me down the coast, eyed me rather suspiciously.

Later in the day I had an early dinner at a local fish joint. It wasn't what you would call elegant, but I wouldn't have felt comfortable dining alone at a fancy restaurant. I then went back to my hotel room and fell asleep watching old movies on cable TV.

The next day, with no particular itinerary planned, I decided to visit Dana Point, another of the towns that had caught my fancy while looking at that virtual map of the United States. The train or bus didn't go directly there, so I had to take the Amtrak to San Juan Capistrano, and from there catch a taxi.

When I got off the train I went into a bar up the street, and asked the woman behind the bar if there was a taxi service close by. The woman said there weren't any nearby, but gave me the number for one that she said would probably pick me up.

I found a phone at the train station, put a quarter in, dialed the number, and received an automated message stating that the call could not be completed until I deposited the correct amount of money. Unfortunately, no instructions followed as to what the correct amount of money would be! I dialed the number a few more times but each time got the same message.

I was starting to feel a bit tense, and called information to try to get the number of a local cab company. They gave me the number for *Yellow Cab of California*. I called Yellow Cab, told them I was at the train station in San Juan Capistrano and wanted to go to Dana Point. The dispatcher said he would check to see if he had any taxis available. We then got cut off and I had to call him back. He told me he had no taxis available at the moment, but was going to call every cab company in the area to find a ride for me, and I should just wait there. I thought his determination to locate a cab for me was a bit strange, but decided I would just wait there as he suggested. A taxi arrived about twenty-minutes later, which ended up being from his company.

The driver was a young man with long hair that reminded me of my hippie days. I sensed there was something very kind about him as I entered the taxi, yet inexplicably, I still felt on edge. He asked me my name, and when I said Richard Kendall he asked if that was the same name as the guy in the television series, *The Fugitive*. I said no, and that the name he was thinking of was Richard Kimball, not Kendall. He then asked in a joking manner if I was also a fugitive. I knew he was just kidding around and trying to make conversation, but the question was unsettling.

The taxi ride from the train station to the harbor at Dana Point was much shorter than I had expected; only about five miles. After dropping me off the driver gave me a card with the cab company's number, and he wrote his name on the back. He said to make sure I asked for him when I was ready to leave. I told him I would. His name was Herb.

The next Amtrak train back to Oceanside from San Juan Capistrano was at 3:15PM. The train after that left at 8:15PM. It was about 1:30 and I figured I'd spend the rest of the day at Dana Point, have dinner there, and take the 8:15 train back.

The harbor at Dana Point was certainly picturesque, but the sense of unease that had begun shortly after I had gotten off the train at San Juan Capistrano kept growing within me. I didn't feel that I was in any kind of physical danger, but I was becoming more and more anxious as each minute passed. This was in such opposition to the sense of calm I had been feeling all week, and I just couldn't get a handle on what was going on.

Although I had only spent about twenty minutes at the harbor, I was still feeling uneasy and called the cab company to have Herb pick me up. This way, I could make the 3:15 train instead of the 8:15, and that would be that. The dispatcher asked if Herb knew where to meet me, and I said to have him pick me up right where he had dropped me off. He said to hold the line while he contacted Herb, and quickly came back on the line to say Herb would be there in about fifteen minutes.

But after hanging up the phone I realized there was a problem. I couldn't remember where Herb had dropped me off! The harbor was fairly large, and if I couldn't remember within the next fifteen minutes and get to that spot, Herb and I would probably miss each other. If that became the case, then I'd be stuck at Dana Point for another five hours until the next train was due to depart. In the frame of mind I was in, the thought of being stuck at Dana Point for another five hours was far from inviting.

All of a sudden, the feelings of anxiousness that had been dogging me all afternoon suddenly exploded into full-blown panic. I began to feel disoriented and at one point I was flat out running through the harbor, trying to get my bearings. It then dawned on me that I could pick out the name of one of the restaurants at the harbor, call the cab company back, and they could radio Herb to meet me there. That realization helped ease my sense of panic, though I was still extremely anxious. I told myself to try to relax, and started to recognize a few restaurants that seemed familiar. I then walked by a shop called *Meara's Pearls*, which I remembered seeing on the way in. Using Meara's Pearls as a reference point, I continued walking to where I thought Herb might have originally dropped me off. (I subsequently found out that Lynda and Stan had visited Dana Point many times, and Lynda had bought jewelry from Meara's Pearls.)

As I continued walking I suddenly saw Herb at the light right across the street. He saw me at the same time and started waving vigorously as if to reassure me everything was going to be okay. He pulled up and seemed genuinely concerned about me. He asked why I was going back so soon and I made up some story that was obviously bullshit, but he went along with it so as not to embarrass me. I kept jabbering about all kinds of inane things, and then, uncharacteristically, I started telling Herb about the Seth material.

I rarely start telling someone about Seth out of the blue but Herb was really impressed by the fact that the material was being housed at Yale University. He said that fact alone gave it an aura of credibility. The fare was a little over nine dollars and I gave him a twenty and told him to keep the change. He thanked me and again asked for my name, which I gave to him. I then asked him for his last name and it was something like Bocker. And that was my day at Dana Point.

On the last day of my Carlsbad vacation I wandered into a store called *Lynda's Gift*. When I first saw the sign, I wondered if in some way this vacation represented a gift from Lynda to me, or was it a gift from me to her. But the distinction didn't matter for when we give to others both giver and receiver share in the exchange.

As I thought about my experiences over the past week, and the connections I felt between Lynda, Stan, and myself, I had concerns about intruding upon a private relationship—yet on some level I felt I had their permission. There were moments when it seemed I was feeling Stan's love for Lynda, and his sense of missing her. During this vacation I received an email from Lynda doing no more than just bringing me up to date as to some of her recent activities, but the email brought tears to my eyes.

As I tried to piece together various elements of my vacation, one of the thoughts that came to mind was that perhaps Stan borrowed a corner of my consciousness to revisit some places which held significant emotional relevance for him during the time he and Lynda had lived together in southern California. His own kind of *Sentimental Journey*, with me as a conduit. And each of us would have participated in the event for our own reasons.

While finishing my bowl of Cheerios and milk that September evening in 1999, I believe Stan and I for a few moments danced a dance of consciousness, which then continued during my Carlsbad vacation. It was a small dance; perhaps a minuet, and I was happy to let him lead.

As I was boarding the plane back to New York City, I thought of my California self standing on the corner of Mendocino and South El Camino Real, waiting for Stan and Lynda to whisk me away. If you see me there, for Christ's sake, please stop and pick me up. But don't do it for Christ's sake; do it for mine.

SHORT STORIES

Sally, BarkRite and The Fortune Cookie

Sally was a very talented actress, and while confident in her acting abilities, she had little confidence when it came to making decisions. As a result, she was always running to psychics for answers. Sally would become particularly agitated when questions arose concerning her career, and on such occasions it was not unusual for her to consult with two or three psychics before taking any action.

One Sunday morning, Sally received a call from her agent regarding a television commercial she had auditioned for earlier in the week. He was pleased to inform her that she had been chosen from a large pool of actresses to introduce to the world a new brand of dog food called *BarkRite*. While not exactly the kind of part an actor dreams of, commercials could be lucrative, and exposure for an actor was something always to be welcomed.

This type of a decision was a no-brainer, and Sally told her agent to call back the *BarkRite* people and tell them she was pleased they had chosen her to represent their dog food and would be available to shoot the commercial at their convenience. An added plus was the fact that the commercial was going to be shot in New York City, where Sally lived. It was one of those instances where everything seemed to fall into place. But as they say, the plot thickens.

Later that week, there was a message on Sally's answering machine. It was from her agent and all he said was that he had some REALLY BIG NEWS, and she should call him back as soon as she got his message. Sally of course called back immediately. The news was that through one of his contacts on the west coast he was able to arrange an audition for her; but this time we weren't talking about a dog food commercial. This was an audition for a major motion picture! Though the part would be relatively small, Sally knew that even a minor appearance in a major motion picture could jumpstart an actor's career. Her agent also found out that the only other actress being seriously considered for the part kept pushing for a bigger role, and in the process was creating friction between herself and the producer.

Sally was just about to shout hooray when it dawned on her that the audition for the movie was scheduled the same day that the shoot for the dog food commercial was slated to take place. Her agent, in his excitement, obviously hadn't realized this, but this left Sally in a real quandary.

While it would be possible to call the people at *BarkRite* and explain the situation to them, she knew from experience that filming schedules were not to be tampered with lightly. If she asked the *BarkRite* people to postpone shooting for even one day, there was a good chance they would simply replace her with someone else. Her initial instinct was to go to California and audition for the movie, but Sally had little faith in her own instincts.

The next morning, before her first sip of coffee, Sally was busy on the phone setting up appointments with no less than four psychics. She posed the same question to each of them: Should she shoot the *BarkRite* commercial as originally planned, or should she go to California and audition for the movie.

Maria, the first psychic Sally visited, used ordinary playing cards to do her readings. Maria shuffled the cards like an expert poker dealer straight from Las Vegas (and there was more truth in that analogy than her clients probably cared to know). When she turned over the *Jack of Spades* who faces east, Maria said this was a clear indication that the best course of action would be to stay close to the east coast and follow through with the *BarkRite* commercial.

Tony, the next psychic Sally consulted, worked with tea leaves. Tony told her the way the leaves were extending toward the edges of the teacup meant that venturing outward would produce favorable results, and encouraged her to go to California and do the audition. So the score was now tied: *BarkRite*: 1, *California Audition*, 1.

Next up was Paula, who specialized in astrology. Paula pointed out that with Mars moving into Pisces and Saturn coming within one degree orb of her Moon, travel at this time should definitely be avoided. The psychic scoreboard now read *BarkRite*: 2, *California Audition*, 1.

Angela, the last psychic on Sally's list worked with Tarot cards. Angela placed the cards face down on the table in front of her. Sally held her breath as Angela reached down very slowly, as if some divine influence was directing her hand, guiding it through some invisible tunnel that only Angela had access to. One could almost feel the tension in Sally's body as Maria started to turn over the card that in Sally's mind might hold within its four corners the entire fate of her acting career. The card Angela finally turned over was the *Eight of Wands*. The Eight of Wands displays the ship Argo in full sail, signifying an auspicious time for travel. The score was now deadlocked: *BarkRite*: 2, *California Audition*: 2, with Sally stuck in the middle.

Later that evening Sally went out with friends for Chinese food. As she broke open her fortune cookie her heart raced; perhaps the fortune cookie might provide the definitive answer and break the 2–2 tie. The fortune cookie contained the following message: *Trust Your Own Instincts*. "Great," Sally sarcastically thought to herself. "I'm in desperate need of an answer and this is what I get."

After a few days of agonizing over which way to go, Sally decided to stick close to home and do the *BarkRite* commercial. She told her agent of her decision, and while he wasn't very happy about it, he told her he would relay the message to the producer on the west coast. So that was that...well...not quite.

The day before the *BarkRite* commercial was to be shot, Sally received a frantic call from her agent. What had happened was that the actress who was up for the part Sally was going to audition for had a falling out with the producer and they parted company. If Sally was willing to fly out to California tonight, or tomorrow morning at the latest, the producer would still let her audition for the part. While it was not one hundred percent guaranteed she would get the part, it was basically a done deal.

So what did Sally do? I'll tell you. Sally did not fly out to the coast that evening, or the next day, or any other day for that matter. She was simply too stressed out to make travel arrangements to go anywhere. She did however appear in the *BarkRite* commercial and earned a tidy sum of money for her efforts. As to the exposure factor, the commercial did little to advance her career.

It is often said that a short time after eating Chinese food one is hungry again. I have no idea where or how this concept originated, and also don't know whether the same applies to eating a bowl of *BarkRite*. But what I do know is that any dog knows the wisdom of Trusting Its Own Instincts. And hopefully one day Sally will learn this also.

The *BarkRite* venture ended up all bark and no bite as the company folded after one year. But the movie Sally was going to audition for was a different story. It was nominated for two Academy Awards and was a major box office success both here and abroad. And ironically the word "Instinct" appears in the film's title. I know you can figure it out. Just trust your basic instincts.

Fat Boy Billy

Fat Boy Billy lived in a small town in the Midwestern part of the United States. Eleven pounds, six ounces at birth, Billy was overweight from day one. As Billy was growing up he saw himself not as a person who was fat, but as a fat person—an important distinction. This fat self-image was reinforced countless times as neighbors and friends simply referred to him as *Fat Boy Billy*. They weren't trying to be mean; the label just seemed to fit.

When Fat Boy Billy was fifteen years old he began to have difficulty at times catching his breath. The doctors told him it was imperative that he lose weight. He stood five feet five inches and weighed 300 pounds. He listened dutifully as well-meaning friends and acquaintances suggested an endless array of diets and disciplines, but he didn't feel motivated by any of them. Then one day he saw this program on television about running.

This fifty-year old woman who had been obese her entire life decided she wanted to see, *to feel*, for once in her life, what it would be like to be thin. She didn't want to do this because of health problems, or because she was concerned with what others thought about how she looked, or to meet some prospective mate. She just wanted for once in her life to know what it would feel like to not be overweight. As Billy listened to her story, her struggles, and her eventual success, he made a decision. The decision was clear—no ifs ands or buts about it—Fat Boy Billy was going to start running, and one day, just like this woman, he too would look in the mirror and see a thin person looking back at him.

When he told the local doctor of his decision to start jogging, there was a moment of disbelief, followed by a stern warning that in light of the shortness of breath episodes he had been experiencing, such an endeavor could prove dangerous. The doctor also told him, with all good intentions, that before he even started thinking about any kind of strenuous exercise he first needed to lose some weight. He went on to suggest a diet that would help him do so. Lastly, he cautioned Billy that since it was the middle of winter, he'd be better off waiting until spring before attempting to do this.

But Fat Boy Billy had made up his mind! He told his grandfather of his decision and his grandfather said he would help Billy in whatever way he could. (Billy's parents had died in an automobile accident when Billy was five years old and his grandfather was the only family he had left.)

Billy asked his grandfather to clock the distance from their front porch until they reached one mile. That way, Billy would have a definite distance he could use as a measuring post. His grandfather got in the car, told Billy to watch the odometer, and when it reached one mile they found themselves parked in front of old man Backer's hardware store, which stood near the edge of town.

Billy decided his ultimate goal would be to jog two miles; one mile to old man Backer's hardware store, and one mile back to his house. He had no idea of how many weeks or months or even years it might take for him to accomplish this feat, but time didn't matter, for Fat Boy Billy had made up his mind!

On January 11, at precisely six o'clock in the morning, Fat Boy Billy put on two pair of running pants, an extra-large sweatshirt, his red beanie, and the long gray secondhand jacket his grandfather had given him. He didn't bother to check the temperature, for having lived in the Midwest his entire life no one had to tell him how cold it would be.

That first day Billy was only able to jog a total of one-half block before feeling totally exhausted, and being literally sick to his stomach. Add to this the fact that it took a while for him to catch his breath as he walked back to his house, and who would have blamed him if he quit right then and there. But he didn't, for Fat Boy Billy had made up his mind!

This same routine followed for most of the week, but on the fifth day not only did he not feel sick, but he had no trouble catching his breath as he walked back home. He was exhilarated by this fact and was more determined than ever to reach his goal.

On day number eight, Fat Boy Billy jogged one entire block, up from one-half block, a one hundred percent increase in distance. By week number three, Fat Boy Billy had lost 5 pounds and was now running two full blocks a day. As far as he could remember, this was the only time in his life he had ever LOST weight. To say he was ecstatic about this would not be an exaggeration.

By week number five, another 4 pounds disappeared, making eight pounds in all. He was now down to 291 from his original weight of 300. Living in a small town, word began to quickly spread about Fat Boy Billy's jogging, and shopkeepers began to open their stores a little earlier each morning to get a glimpse of him as he jogged by. Many of the townspeople had small apartments above the stores, and they too started getting up a little earlier to watch from their windows as Fat Boy Billy jogged by. By week number ten, Billy was running four blocks a day, had lost 19 pounds in all, and was now down to 281 pounds.

By the beginning of the fourteenth week, April 11 to be exact, the town was buzzing. Fat Boy Billy had not missed a single day of jogging since he began on January 11. *Ninety-one* straight days through rain, snow, and temperatures that often dipped below zero. But the weather conditions didn't matter, because Fat Boy Billy had made up his mind!

Every morning, on went the two pair of running pants, extra-large sweatshirt, long gray secondhand jacket, and red beanie. By week sixteen a number of the townsfolk began to shout words of encouragement from their windows overlooking the street as Billy passed by.

As the first few days of May came around, Billy had lost 30 pounds, and was now down to 270. But equally important to Billy, for the first time he had run one full mile! As all accomplishments are relative, being able to run one full mile made Billy feel as if he was on his way to winning an Olympic Gold Medal.

As spring finally began to take hold and the weather began to warm, Billy not only shed more pounds, but shed some clothes as well. He now dressed in one pair of running pants, one long sleeve pullover, and though he didn't really need it, he kept the red beanie on his head. It just made him feel good to put it on before starting his run each morning.

Without even thinking about it, Billy was also eating far less than usual. It was now June 11, and Billy had lost 8 more pounds. Everyone in town was beginning to wonder if a miracle was unfolding before their eyes. Every morning as Billy passed by you could hear the chants of 'Go Billy Go! Go Billy Go!' He heard them, and felt them, but he never looked up, and his expression never changed.

By the time mid-August rolled around, Fat Boy Billy had lost 50 pounds, and from mid-August through the end of September, Billy lost another 4 pounds. A total of 54 pounds had departed for points unknown since Billy had begun, and his weight was now down to 246.

On October 9, a panting Fat Boy Billy jogged two miles for the first time. Despite the chill in the morning air, the chants of "Go Billy Go!" were louder than ever. October 9 to December 19, jogging two miles a day now, Billy lost another 9 pounds, now weighing in at 237 from his starting weight of 300.

On Christmas morning, the town quietly watched the familiar sight of Fat Boy Billy in his red beanie jogging to old man Backer's hardware store and back. No shouts of 'Go Billy Go' filled the air that morning. Everyone seemed to realize that Billy was running not only for himself, not only to lose weight, but was running for everyone in town, carrying with him their own unspoken dreams with his every step.

Eight more pounds were shed from December 19 to January 16. Billy's weight was now down to 229. On March 30, Billy finally cracked the 200 pound barrier, as the scale registered 199 pounds. April ran its course as 8 more pounds disappeared in the cool morning air. The warm winds of May and June helped dissolve another 12 pounds.

On July 24, at the town's annual picnic dinner, when Billy was asked to say a few words, a 175-pound Billy walked up to the microphone. As he looked out at everyone and heard the thunderous applause, tears came to his eyes and he couldn't speak. He didn't have to. He knew he never could have done it without them, and they knew it too.

Jonathan and Lavinia

Jonathan and Lavinia met one night at a New Year's Eve party hosted by a friend of Jonathan's. They were briefly introduced, exchanged a few words, and that was the extent of their interaction for the evening. Yet Jonathan felt an immediate connection with Lavinia which he couldn't explain. And Lavinia felt the same way toward Jonathan. Their feelings may have stemmed in part from an unconscious recognition that they both suffered from an extreme case of very low self-esteem. This poor self-image led each of them to expect rejection at every turn.

As the week progressed, Jonathan found himself thinking more and more about Lavinia and decided to ask his friend for Lavinia's phone number. For many of us such a request would be of little import, but for Jonathan, asking for Lavinia's phone number was no small feat. Emailing her certainly would have been easier, but personal computing was in its early stages at the time and the telephone still reigned supreme.

Lavinia was surprised that Jonathan wanted to get in touch with her, but was also delighted. She gave out her number and waited for Jonathan to call. Jonathan waited too. He got Lavinia's number on a Tuesday, and it took him the rest of the week to find the resolve to actually dial it. As Jonathan was struggling to find the strength within himself to make that call, Lavinia's heart raced every time she heard the phone ring, hoping it would be Jonathan.

Saturday morning, as the coffee was almost done brewing, Lavinia put a slice of that raisin bread she liked so well into the toaster. Being able to sleep late on Saturday, and have a cup of freshly brewed coffee with the newspaper spread out before her was a ritual Lavinia always looked forward to. Just as she took her first sip of coffee the phone rang. She jumped up and had a strong feeling it was Jonathan. But when she picked up the receiver, much to her dismay, the voice on the other end of the phone belonged to her mother.

Lavinia usually spoke to her mother once a week; it took the other six days to recover. Her mother's level of expertise at being able to push Lavinia's buttons was unparalleled. Today, her mother was really on, repeatedly hitting the target head on with the precision of an expert marksman. Unfortunately, the target was another human being, and one with fragile feelings to boot.

While trying to hold back all the anger that was building up inside of her, Lavinia heard a beep indicating that another caller was trying to get through. She put her mother on hold and without even asking who it was just blurted out "Call back later," with obvious annoyance in her voice. While Jonathan didn't expect Lavinia to sing a chorus of *Joy To The World* upon hearing his voice, a short (and not so sweet) "Call back later," was just too much. He felt devastated. The only words he was able to get out was a barely audible "This is Jonathan," after which he promptly hung up the phone.

It took a few moments to register, but when Lavinia realized what had just happened she quickly ended the 'discussion' with her mother and sat by the phone waiting for Jonathan to call back. She told herself that when he called back she would explain why she answered the phone in the way that she did, and they could move on from there.

The situation however was not that simple. For one thing, it never occurred to Jonathan that Lavinia had someone else on hold, and while he might have paused to wonder if there was a reason why she answered the phone in such a brusque manner, his insecurities took over as they had done so many times before. He was much too upset to try to rationally sort out what had just happened.

As Lavinia sat by the phone eagerly awaiting Jonathan's call, anticipation turned to worry. From there it took no more than the blink of an eye for Lavinia to retreat into the same negative patterns of thought she had set in motion a thousand times before.

It was clear to Lavinia that once again she was being rejected. At this point in her life her perception of rejection and the fact of actually being rejected had become one and the same. She never considered the possibility that at times she might be misinterpreting circumstances so as to fit her preconceived belief in the inevitability of her being rejected.

She concluded that Jonathan was never all that interested in her to begin with, for otherwise he surely would have called back. And in line with Jonathan's low self-esteem, he concluded that Lavinia probably gave out her number just to be polite, with no real desire to get together with him. With such a rejection-oriented mindset shared by both of them, what might have been the start of a meaningful relationship came to an abrupt end before it had a chance to begin.

Over the next year Jonathan and Lavinia had no contact, but found themselves thinking a lot about the fact that they weren't getting any younger and didn't want to spend the rest of their lives alone. So when the opportunity to marry presented itself, they each leapt at the chance. And while neither marriage proved to be very fulfilling, the mere fact that someone was willing to spend the rest of their lives with them brought with it some degree of satisfaction.

One evening, with their respective mates at their side, Jonathan and Lavinia happened to meet outside a movie theater. Between the obligatory introductions and minor chitchat that followed, there was a moment when their eyes locked. In that moment, it was as if they were transported to another dimension, *standing under a light of crystal clear comprehension*. The realization that an opportunity had passed them by flooded their minds, and sent minor shockwaves throughout their bodies.

As they returned to their usual state of consciousness, all that was left to do was to say their goodbyes, wish each other luck, and walk away with the knowledge that they would never see or hear from each other again.

Yet at times, late at night, that moment outside the movie theater comes back to haunt them; lingers for a few moments, and then disappears like some half-remembered dream, as do their lives.

George

George was an only child whose father died when George was only ten years old. His mother never remarried, and firmly shut all doors regarding the possibility of meeting another man. From the day her husband died, all her energies were focused on one object, or shall we say subject; her son George. She was endlessly attentive, always rushing to do things for George, and prided herself on always being there for him.

George was tall, thin, and walked with his head always lowered a bit, as if making eye contact with others might spark off some unspeakable catastrophe. George was also not very coordinated. He never quite felt connected to his body; as if somehow it was separate from him, like some distant relative who he would only see on special occasions.

His overall demeanor made him a perfect target for bullies, and he resigned himself to the daily dose of ridicule that would come his way each day at school. If he had a particularly bad day, George's mother had an uncanny ability to sense this, and would console him with the following words: "Don't' worry George, whatever happens, your mother will always be there for you."

As George got older and made his way through high school, the bullying and the ridicule subsided significantly. He was seen by others simply as some weirdo who kept to himself, and no one bothered with him much one way or the other.

As far as girls were concerned, George rarely dated, and the few times he did, he was so shy that any kind of a relationship never had a chance to develop. And when he did go out on a date, his mother would always tell him that he shouldn't expect too much; and not to worry if the girl didn't want to see him again.

Whenever the opportunity arose, (and often enough when it didn't) George's mother would continue to remind him: "Don't worry George, whatever happens, your mother will always be there for you."

When high school ended George took a job at the local Post Office, continued to live at home, and while life wasn't very exciting, at the same time there was little to complain about. Being accepted by his coworkers was in itself a big plus for George, considering the constant ridicule he received while growing up. After five years of working at the Post

Office, George rose to the rank of Supervisor. And if he had a bad day, or seemed troubled by something, his mother always found the time to speak the words she had spoken a thousand times before to him: "Don't worry George, whatever happens, your mother will always be there for you."

By now I'm sure it's no surprise that one wouldn't consider George a passionate person, and yet, he did have one passion in life—movies. George LOVED movies. A week didn't go by when he didn't purchase at least one new videotape, (this was pre-dvd and streaming days), and George watched them all. He could tell you what actor or actress played some bit part in some obscure movie from twenty years ago, as well as what they had appeared in since.

One day while George was helping a young man track a lost shipment of videotapes at the Post Office, they struck up a conversation regarding old movies. Despite the fact that this fellow was only in his mid-twenties, he told George that in the next few months he was going to open a chain of video rental stores in the Chicago area called *The Moving Image*. He already had signed leases for two stores and was hoping to expand over time into other parts of the country. Right now though he needed someone with organizational skills and a love of movies to supervise the two stores in Chicago. He asked George if he would be interested in discussing with him the possibility of George filling the position.

Except for an occasional daydream, George never thought much about leaving the Post Office, and yet, surprising himself, he agreed to have lunch with this fellow. Just having someone who felt as passionate as he did about movies was excuse enough to get together.

George didn't mention any of this to his mother for he didn't want to unnecessarily upset her. He also felt extremely guilty at even considering the idea of taking this job. What kind of a selfish monster would leave his aging mother after all the years she had devoted to him. On the other hand, George also found himself thinking, Chicago was not the end of the world; he could get on a plane and be home within a few hours.

So he kept his lunch date with the owner of *The Moving Image*, who was so impressed by George's knowledge and enthusiasm about movies, that he offered George the job on the spot. Never one to act impulsively, George said he would think it over and let him know within the next few days.

The next day George decided he had to tell his mother about the lunch date he had with this fellow and the opportunity that was offered him. As expected, his mother did not react well. "You have security at the Post Office; all kinds of benefits; paid holidays; a pension that increases every year. How can you take such a risk when there is no guarantee that this fellow's business won't fall apart soon after it starts, and where will that leave you. And what do you know about this person. Where would such a young man get that much money anyway?"

George felt like he was being pulled with equal force in two completely opposite directions. His mother was right about the security he had at the Post Office. Did it really make sense to take such a chance on a job that might end as quickly as it began. So George called his would-be employer, thanked him for the opportunity, and life went back to normal.

Over the next year George didn't think much about the job offer that had come his way, but one morning when reading one of his video news magazines, he came across an interview with the president of *The Moving Image*, the same fellow he had met with for lunch that day.

The article mentioned that *The Moving Image* was now the number one movie rental chain in the Chicago area, and new stores would soon be opening in Milwaukee before the end of the year. George was pleased for the owner's success, but what was done was done. All in all, life wasn't that bad George told himself. Others had it far worse than him and he should be grateful for what he did have.

As the years went by, George found himself growing more and more irritable and impatient with his mother. Her tendency to complain about the same things over and over again using the exact same words to do so could be difficult to take at times. But he chalked it up to her becoming older and told himself he needed to be more patient.

One Sunday morning, while reading his video magazine, George saw a blurb about *The Moving Image.* It wasn't an interview with the owner but simply stated that *The Moving Image* was in talks with Paramount Pictures about starting a joint venture that could lead to over a hundred new stores opening up in various parts of the country within the next two years.

George spent the rest of the day at the baseball stadium watching a doubleheader. The Post Office often received free tickets for sporting events and when some coworker had to cancel out, the ticket went to George. The first game was a classic pitcher's duel with the visiting team winning by one run. The second game wasn't very exciting as the home team was getting trounced.

George left early to beat the traffic, and when he got home that evening, his mother, as always, had dinner waiting. He sat down at the table, and with his mother sitting across from him they each began to eat the homemade tomato soup which both of them liked so well. George made a comment about how good the soup was, and his mother, pleased that he was enjoying the soup, looked up at him and started to repeat the same phrase that she had uttered countless times before: "Whatever happens George … but before she could finish, George ERUPTED! His mother couldn't make out half of what he was saying— something about Paramount Pictures, and Chicago, and movies.

She was so startled and frightened by his behavior she didn't know what to think. Could he have eaten something bad at the ball game, or could there have been something in the tomato soup that was causing this strange behavior. Should she call the police, the doctor, the hospital. She just stood there trembling, not knowing what to do.

After a few moments, while heaving great sobs, George slowly walked to his room. His mother waited a few minutes, tiptoed into the room and sat down next to him on the bed. She fluffed his pillow, took off his shoes, and tucked him into bed. "Try to get some rest," she told him. "Don't worry about sleeping in your clothes; I'll wash them in the morning." She then paused a few moments as George just lay there staring up at the ceiling, and said "Don't worry George, whatever happens, your mother will always be there for you." And though she hated wasting food, just in case she threw out the rest of the tomato soup.

The next day George went back to work, the mail got delivered on time, and the earth continued to follow the same orbit around the sun that it had traversed for centuries. A couple of things did change however. For one, George's mother decided never to make tomato soup again. She felt she just couldn't take the chance. And George decided not to renew his subscription to the video magazine he had regularly been reading for the past few years.

When George's mother died, he looked at her in the open casket and a part of him half-expected to see her lips move, and speak the words, "Don't worry George, your mother will always be there for you." The other part of him knew he would never hear those words again.

He then went home, made his own dinner, and though his mother was gone, all in all, life wasn't so bad. Plenty of others had it much worse than him he reminded himself. He even went back to eating tomato soup on occasion. And while it wasn't as good as his mother's homemade tomato soup, it wasn't all that bad either. How much could one expect out of life, anyway. In George's case, very little—and his expectations were fully met. They always are.

MISCELLANEOUS

Free As A Bird

The other morning while I was looking out the window I noticed a Blue Jay sitting in front of my garage and not moving. I went out and started to walk toward it, and when I began to get too close to it, the Blue Jay hopped a short distance away, yet made no attempt at flight. I wondered if the bird was injured. As I started to walk toward it again, the bird flew into a nearby tree. I thought its behavior was a bit odd, but was happy to see the Blue Jay was alright.

About ten minutes later I happened to look out the window again and saw the Blue Jay once more sitting near the garage. I went out and the same routine was repeated. When I got too close, the Blue Jay flew away. I figured that was the end of the story. But as I glanced out my window about fifteen minutes later, once again there sat the Blue Jay. But this time, rather than sitting in front of the garage, it was sitting in a patch of grass just outside my door. It sat motionless with its wings outstretched. I then knew that the bird was preparing to die.

I wondered what thoughts or images might have been present in the Blue Jay's mind. Was it reliving some of its great exuberant flights through the trees, when its loud squawking announced to the world the reality and rightness of its existence. Or maybe it was remembering the delight of devouring some particularly juicy worm it had caught one autumn morning. And then again, perhaps it was simply focused in the moment, looking out at the trees and the sky as it had done a thousand times before, despite the knowledge of its impending death.

I don't know what the Blue Jay was thinking, but there was something majestic about the way it sat there with its wings spread out, acquiescing to the inevitable with such grace and dignity. I went back into the house and about five minutes later when I looked out the window I saw the bird lying on its side. It obviously had passed over.

I thought about how this amazing creature, this unique materialization of consciousness had lived its life; so different from the way I was living mine. During its lifetime it trusted its instincts without question. The Blue Jay never worried it might be headed in the wrong direction, or making a mistake. It just flew.

Holding the Blue Jay gently in my hands I walked toward the back of the house and placed it in the middle of some tall grass. I thought the spot I chose would be a perfect place for it to *rest in peace*. Yet as soon as that cliché crossed my mind I realized it didn't fit. Resting in peace was not what characterized the life of that Blue Jay, nor would it characterize its life after its death.

I thanked the Blue Jay for sharing its last moments on earth with me, and as I wondered what new skies it was already soaring through, another cliché came to mind which fit a lot better: *Free as a bird.*

Vive la différence

Seth once said: *"In your terms now and using your terms, an imaginative event is as real as a physically materialized one."*

With that quote in mind, let me share with you the following imaginative encounter.

A few summers ago I spent some time visiting the city of Valencia, off the coast of Spain. Valencia draws thousands of tourists year round, and is known for its magnificent architecture, numerous cultural attractions, and ancient monuments dating back many centuries. After visiting the old monuments in the town's historic district, I stopped for lunch at one of the open-air cafes overlooking the Mediterranean Sea. As I was savoring the taste of coconut rum and pineapple juice, I noticed this woman sitting at the table across from me. I don't know how I missed seeing her before because she was quite striking.

She had long black silken hair, deep blue eyes the color of the nearby ocean, and though probably in her early sixties, radiated that special kind of beauty that no doubt she had possessed her entire life. I found myself quite drawn to her, and staring a bit longer than might be considered polite. Just as I was about to turn my head away she caught my eye and smiled. It was such a warm and natural smile, unlike the contrived or forced smiles one often sees during the course of their day. She then motioned for me to join her.

I picked up my drink, walked over to her table and sat down. I introduced myself and she responded in kind, telling me her name was Miss Di Versity, Do you know the origin of the word diversity? she asked. I told her I did not. She went on to explain. "It's from the Latin *diversitas*, meaning difference," she said. She told me she believed that the creation of our world came from the need to diversify, from a deep yearning to break free from a sameness that had imprisoned our spirits for eons, and the differences found in all things reflected that original need.

She then looked directly into my eyes and told me to imagine a world where everyone was the same. Imagine, she said, if every single person on this earth looked exactly the same, dressed exactly the same, walked exactly the same, and spoke exactly the same. Living in such a world would become more painful to inhabit than we might think.

If we all looked exactly alike, she said, we'd become invisible to each other, as well as to ourselves. And if we all spoke the same, we'd eventually go deaf, for all voices would blend together in one long endless tone. And if everyone dressed exactly the same, the world would become like a picture frozen in time, and our eyes would lose their curiosity and their ability to distinguish differences in shape and color because there would be no differences.

If we ever found ourselves living in such a world of sameness we would understand how precious diversity is. She paused for a few moments, and I felt like she wanted to give me some time to digest the words she had just spoken.

She then continued: Seek not to punish diversity or destroy it, but be thankful you live in a world of differences. Be proud of your own unique nature, and create space in your mind to appreciate the unique nature of all others.

She then gracefully got up from the table, and without saying another word started to walk away. As if on cue some street musician began to play a Brazilian melody that I was familiar with but couldn't remember the title.

I continued to sip my drink, and as I looked about I was struck by all the colors and smells and shapes and sounds that surrounded me. I realized that these were just a tiny fraction of an endless diversity that occupied every corner of the planet. How did such limitless diversity come about I wondered. What kind of being could possess such a massive imagination. The answer to that question didn't really matter at the moment, for I was absorbed with noticing all the endless nuances that while ever-changing still fit together to form a perfect picture of the world.

*** As I was doing some minor editing on the above piece I decided to call it quits for the night and watch a movie. I had an impulse to finish watching a movie on Netflix that I had started a few days ago. It was called *The Country Teacher*, written and directed by Bohdan Slama from The Czech Republic.

I had watched most of it so there were only a few scenes left. In one of those scenes, the teacher is speaking to his students and says the following: *"Imagine how awful it would be if we were all the same."* The line in the movie mirrored exactly the sentiments that I was just writing about in the above piece.

Vereingung der Seth-Freunde

On October 31, 2008, I attended a four-day international Seth conference in Pforzheim, Germany. The conference was organized by Vereingung der Seth-Freunde. (Info @sethfreunde.org) and I was invited there as a guest speaker due to the fact that I had attended Jane Roberts' ESP classes during the 1970's. Having been to other Seth conferences, I knew I'd encounter a variety of viewpoints and interpretations in regards to the Seth material, as well as a number of different approaches to the exploration of consciousness in general. It can be quite challenging at times to listen to others present ideas that differ sharply from your own, and not have your buttons pushed. That is a challenge I continue to work on with varying degrees of success.

When I walked into the main conference room that first day I was greeted by the following comment, "Are you *the one*?" I was literally taken aback, and didn't know how to respond, nor was I quite sure exactly what I'd be responding to! What I did know for sure was that I was not *Neo* from The *Matrix*, so as far as being "the one" it was easy to rule that one out. I then realized that the questioner was referring to the fact that I was "the one" who had participated in Jane Roberts' classes and would be sharing some of those experiences during the course of the conference.

A few moments later, I found myself standing between two people who were discussing the notes that Robert F. Butts, Jane's husband, had inserted into many of the Seth books. One woman said that she found the notes totally useless and just skipped over them. The other woman stated that she loved reading those notes and thought they were an excellent addition to the material.

I then wandered over to some table where various translations of the Seth books were on display. I turned around and almost bumped into this woman whom I hadn't noticed was standing so close behind me. Without introducing herself or engaging in any preliminary introduction of any kind, she promptly informed me that Seth was now channeling through someone in Düsseldorf. She went on to tell me that the resulting material was not as distorted as the material produced by Jane Roberts when she was "the one" speaking for Seth.

I politely told her that Seth had made a point at the beginning of the sessions that he would not speak through anyone else but Jane so as to keep the integrity of the material intact, and avoid the exact kind of situation this woman was now describing. In reaction to my comment she became quite indignant. She told me in no uncertain terms that *she was seventy-six years old and knew what was real and what was not.*

I was curious as to why the ability to see things clearly occurred at one's seventy-sixth birthday, as opposed to their seventy-fifth, or seventy-fourth for that matter, but kept such sarcasm to myself. As she continued to support her position with increasing vehemence, it became obvious that there was no point in discussing this further. I exited as gracefully as possible, while muttering some unflattering words under my breath.

At another point in the conference, someone stood up and proclaimed that Jane's health problems stemmed from the fact that Seth bombarded Jane with too much information, and that although Jane wanted to stop the sessions, Seth was insistent that they continue. That statement, while untrue, was an extreme example of something I would be reminded of many times during the course of the weekend: EVERYONE, (every person on this planet) was going to view reality in their own individual way, filter their experiences through the lens of their own beliefs, and then develop their own set of "facts" in response.

On Saturday, along with about twenty other people, I attended a workshop that was conducted by Ritchie Dvorak. Ritchie was the one, or shall I say the person, who officially invited me to the conference. He and his wife Gudren were also gracious enough to allow me to stay at their home during my time in Germany.

The first thing Ritchie did during his workshop was to lead us in a visualization. After the visualization we all spoke about what we saw, and then the fun really began. There was a canvas about fifteen feet long and four feet high that stretched across the wall. Near it there was a table filled with all kinds of paints and colored chalks. Each of us was to paint the scene we remembered from our visualization. We were also told that we shouldn't worry about whether we were a good artist or a bad artist, and there was no right or wrong way to do this. I was relieved to hear that, for doodling odd shapes and images was the extent to which my artistic abilities extended.

So I picked a corner of the canvas and began painting this house I saw during my visualization. The house was coming out a bit crooked and tilted on its side, but I was sure the stick-figure people I was drawing who were about to take up residence wouldn't mind at all. All the while I was painting I was enjoying a delicious sense of freedom, unconcerned as to how my picture was going to stack up against the other pictures that were being painted. In short, my self-worth was not tied in to the results of my efforts.

When I finished painting and looked around at all the other pictures, it became clear to me that no matter how much each picture differed, there was room enough for each of us to paint our individual pictures of reality without intruding upon the pictures that others were painting.

As I was sitting on the plane going back to the states I started to think about that seventy-six year old lady who had looked me straight in the eye and told me that she knew that this other Seth in Dusseldorf was "the real thing," In hindsight, (ah, the wisdom of hindsight) I wished I had responded differently, less abruptly, while still feeling free to honestly express my opinion.

In hindsight I realized I had missed something very important in the exchange that took place between me and that woman. I was so caught up in defending my own picture of reality, that I missed seeing the reality of the person standing right in front of me—a person who at seventy-six years old still had the grit and perseverance to keep searching for answers. I missed seeing the courage of an individual who was still exploring the mysteries of life, unwilling to accept ready-made versions of reality handed down to us like some mass produced tube of toothpaste coming off an assembly line.

Whether Seth was actually speaking through someone in Dusseldorf or retired in Florida sipping Piña Coladas by the ocean, I missed an opportunity to connect with a lady who probably could have shared some fascinating stories about her life; stories I will now never know.

Jane Roberts once said that if you begin to see people merely as beliefs, instead of as individuals who *hold* various beliefs, then you have really lost something valuable in your interactions with others. I *had* lost something valuable, and while I had to travel a long way to recover it, the trip was well worth it!

Memories of Jane

I gave the following presentation at a Seth Conference in Seaside, Oregon in April of 1996.

I want to tell you about a woman I knew who grew up on welfare; was kicked out of college; went cross-country on a motorcycle; married and divorced three years later; smoked; drank wine and beer; and at times swore like a sailor. Her name was Jane Roberts.

Shortly before Jane died, she told Rob, "DON'T LET THEM MAKE A GOD OUT OF ME." So I hope that by providing some details of Jane's personal life, both before and after Seth emerged, you will be able to see her more clearly as the very *human* being she was. Yet her accomplishments in the field of consciousness exploration spring from that same humanity, so I will also include examples of her often remarkable abilities.

Jane was born in 1929 and grew up in Saratoga Springs, New York. Her parents divorced when she was three years old, and Jane lived with her mother, Marie, who was an invalid.

"I once tried to poison the welfare lady, Jane recalls. I took Brillo and Comet and mixed it in with the hot chocolate and set it down. My mother must have known from my face that something was up. This woman had a beautiful white suit on and my mother said, 'Mrs. Calkins, I wouldn't drink that if I were you. I don't like the look on my daughter's face.' And the welfare lady said, 'Oh, she's the loveliest girl, Marie.' So she took a sip and promptly spit it up."

When Jane was about six, her mother became completely bedridden as a result of an acute arthritic condition. It then became Jane's responsibility to take care of her, which included cooking, cleaning, bringing her the bedpan, and getting up in the middle of the night to refuel the stove. Her mother used to tell Jane that she was going to turn on the gas jets in the middle of the night, and kill them both.

"My mother was a real bitch," Jane says, "but she was an energetic bitch. When my mother attempted suicide for about the fifth time, she took a whole mess of sleeping pills and was in the hospital. I went to the welfare lady and said, 'I can't take it anymore. I've just got to leave.'"

Jane had been going with a fellow named Walt at the time, and they decided to go to California by motorcycle to visit Jane's father. Upon returning to Saratoga Springs Walt and Jane got married. "Three years we lived together," Jane says in an interview. "Then I found out -- while I was working in a radio factory putting lover-boy Walt through school, everybody else in town knew -- he isn't going through school." Then, Jane met Rob:

"I wrote him a poem the second time I met him. The fourth time, it was a party, we'd never kissed, we'd never had a date. I just looked at him and said, 'Look, I'm leaving Walt, and I'm going to leave by myself or I'm going to leave with you, so just let me know." The following excerpt from one of Jane's personal journals, written in 1978, sheds some light on the nature of Jane's relationship with Rob:

"I think, this minute anyhow, that I am lonely; except for Rob, my work or Seth's is so often misunderstood; used for ends that to me are unfortunate, as if somehow despite all Seth says or I say, we are just a slightly more exotic species of the psychic master and his holy sister." This passage reminded me of times when Jane questioned whether her books were really helping anyone. I don't think she was looking for praise or even reassurance, but simply sharing with us some of the doubts she had about the value of the work she was doing.

Over the years, people from all walks of life witnessed Seth speaking. Some went to class for an evening, others attended for longer periods of time. Outside of the class structure, Jane gave many personal Seth sessions to various individuals who had written her asking for help. She never charged for any of those sessions. She did, however, charge $3.50 a class when I first started attending, but when the books began to sell in sufficient numbers, she dropped the fee.

"During class, Jane remained seated in her Kennedy Rocking Chair, but about halfway through class she would always take a break and go across the hall to her other apartment for about fifteen minutes. I remember one particular evening where Jane got up from her rocker to walk across the hall, as I had seen her do so many times before, but for some reason this particular evening it was as if I was watching her do this for the first time. I had never noticed the extreme difficulty she had in getting her legs to move, in just putting one foot in front of the other. It was an impression that never left me.

On the other side of the coin, the speed and dexterity of Jane's mental gymnastics were in sharp contrast to the physical constraints with which she lived. Here is an example of Jane's mobility when it came to her consciousness. This occurred one evening after class had officially ended for the night.

Jane said, "Rich, look at me; now I am Jane." In that moment she was Jane as I knew her in her usual state. Then she closed her eyes for an instant, opened them, and said, "Now I am Sumari." Jane's face now displayed the look and feel of when she sang Sumari, a distinct difference from her usual countenance. Then, closing her eyes again and quickly opening them, she said in her normal voice, "Now I am what you think of as Seth, *without* the voice." I stared with wonder into Seth's eyes as he peered back into mine. Once again Jane closed her eyes, opened them, and Seth said, "Now I am what you think of as Seth *with* the voice!" Jane closed and opened her eyes again, "Now I am something you don't know yet." Eyes closed, opened, and she was back to the usual Jane, who then said, "Do you see the difference?" I had just witnessed a demonstration in the nature of consciousness that lasted all of about 30 seconds, yet a demonstration one could ponder for a lifetime.

Another incident from class that stands out in my mind transpired while Jane was singing Sumari. Her arthritis was so severe that she could not lift her arm over her shoulder, yet while in trance singing Sumari this one evening, she lifted her arm high above her head to everyone's amazement. When she came out of trance, the class informed her of what she had done. Now out of trance, she tried again to lift her arm above her head, but could only lift it to shoulder level.

Another evening when we were once again hanging around after class, Jane looked at Bobby Axelrod, one of the students, and spontaneously gave him the following reincarnational data: She told Bobby that he was a beautiful woman with long black hair with combs in it, and that he lived near Majorca, Spain. He was a highly skilled dancer, and had eight children, five of which were stillborn. He believed in a superstition at the time, that if a stillborn child was buried in the earth, the next would survive. Jane then said that in dancing and acting in this life, Bobby has the ability to easily switch between male and female movements.

So besides not knowing what *Seth* might say at any given moment, we also never knew what *Jane* might come up with: "Rich, you were an Indian," Jane once commented to me, and then just continued with class. Seemingly apropos of nothing, she looked at one of the students one evening and said, "I think you once killed me, yet not from hate but clumsily. It almost seems amusing."

Another time she told the same student that at 14 years old he had picked up an idea about the nature of reality that has held him back sexually. She said a math course and a woman named Sylvia were connected. The student revealed that in 10th grade Geometry he had a teacher whose first name was Sylvia. These are just a few instances of what were no doubt thousands of psychic impressions Jane had during her lifetime. Looking back, I can only wonder at the kinds of things Jane picked up that remained *unspoken*.

When class resumed at the "hill house," as Jane and Rob called their new home, Jane was much more open than she had been before. I remember her talking about some person in class who, in her words, "used to drive me up a wall." Listening to her speak like that surprised me. I guess I was so mesmerized by Seth and so struck by Jane's abilities, that evidence from Jane of the everyday feelings we all experience caught me off guard. One other note along these lines: Jane once told us that if she wanted to she could have had us all wrapped around her finger, but it was an important point in her development not to use her abilities in such a manner.

People came to Jane always wanting something, and add to that the fact that they rarely ever wanted that something from *Jane*, but from *Seth*. Jane mentioned once that she still resented it when new people came to class with the attitude "will Seth come through?"

The Air Force once contacted Jane to see if she could help locate a missing pilot whose plane had crashed while on a training mission in upstate NY. Jane told them she had an impression of the letter M and twin mountains. The pilot was found at Mt. Matumbel. She then picked up so much data about the pilot that the government became suspicious that she may have somehow been involved in the whole incident—an interesting example of what sometimes happens when unofficial abilities meet the official world.

The following passage from one of Jane's personal journals caught my eye recently: "I dreamed that in the future, all households would be connected to interconnecting computers, keeping track of all inhabitants, actions, goods, and so forth." This was written in 1981, long before the Internet became as prevalent as it is today.

The following incident which also occurred in 1981, underscores the great depth of Jane's abilities. I was experiencing some health problems which led me to call Jane. I was not able to speak with her but spoke briefly with Rob, who said he would relay my message. I then took the train to the city to run some errands. While walking around Manhattan I felt a sudden wave of incredibly calm energy encircling my body. It was quite tangible. I didn't connect the experience with my phone call to Jane, since I had not spoken with her.

I returned home about 7:00 PM, and Jane called. She told me that she had tried to reach me by phone numerous times during the afternoon and when unsuccessful, concentrated on sending me energy, imagining it going all over my body. She was very supportive and concerned. I only realized years later the extent of her own health problems at that time, yet in spite of that, she was able and willing to reach out with healing energy for others.

One last experience I'll relate happened in 1978. A friend and I stopped by unannounced to see Jane and Rob. While there, I started telling Jane how I hoped to be able to create my life with high after high, infused with peak experiences just like her life was. I also spoke of wanting to feel part of a meaningful universe.

Without putting down my intent, Jane explained to me that while she did have her highs, her life was *not* an endless series of peak experiences, but was filled with ups and downs just like anyone else's life. Then, quite unexpectedly, Seth came through and said the following: "You are not so much part of a meaningful universe as the universe in part. That is the next step for you to joyfully follow." And I think that is the next step for all of us to joyfully follow. Thank you.

Postcards from Jane Roberts & Robert Butts

Sent to Rich Kendall

POSTCARD ONE - FRONT

This postcard, like most that follow, address me by my nickname, "Dickie," though in this one Jane spelled it with a "y" at the end. I was called Dickie until my early twenties when Dickie finally gave way to Richard.

The drawing on the card was done by Jane

An elegent
old-fashioned purple couch
for people
with purple hair!

Sit on a Royal couch
And comb your purple dreams
And brush your silky thoughts
into magic melodies

Jane

Postcard one - Back

The "purple hair" reference had to do with an ESP Class session dated October 3, 1972.

I believe the "Royal couch" comment referred to reincarnational information given to me by Seth in a class dated March 28, 1972. The information is reproduced in Chapter 8 of *The Road To Elmira,* Volume 1.

The "magic melodies" had to do with the fact that I was devoting a lot of energy at that time toward writing songs.

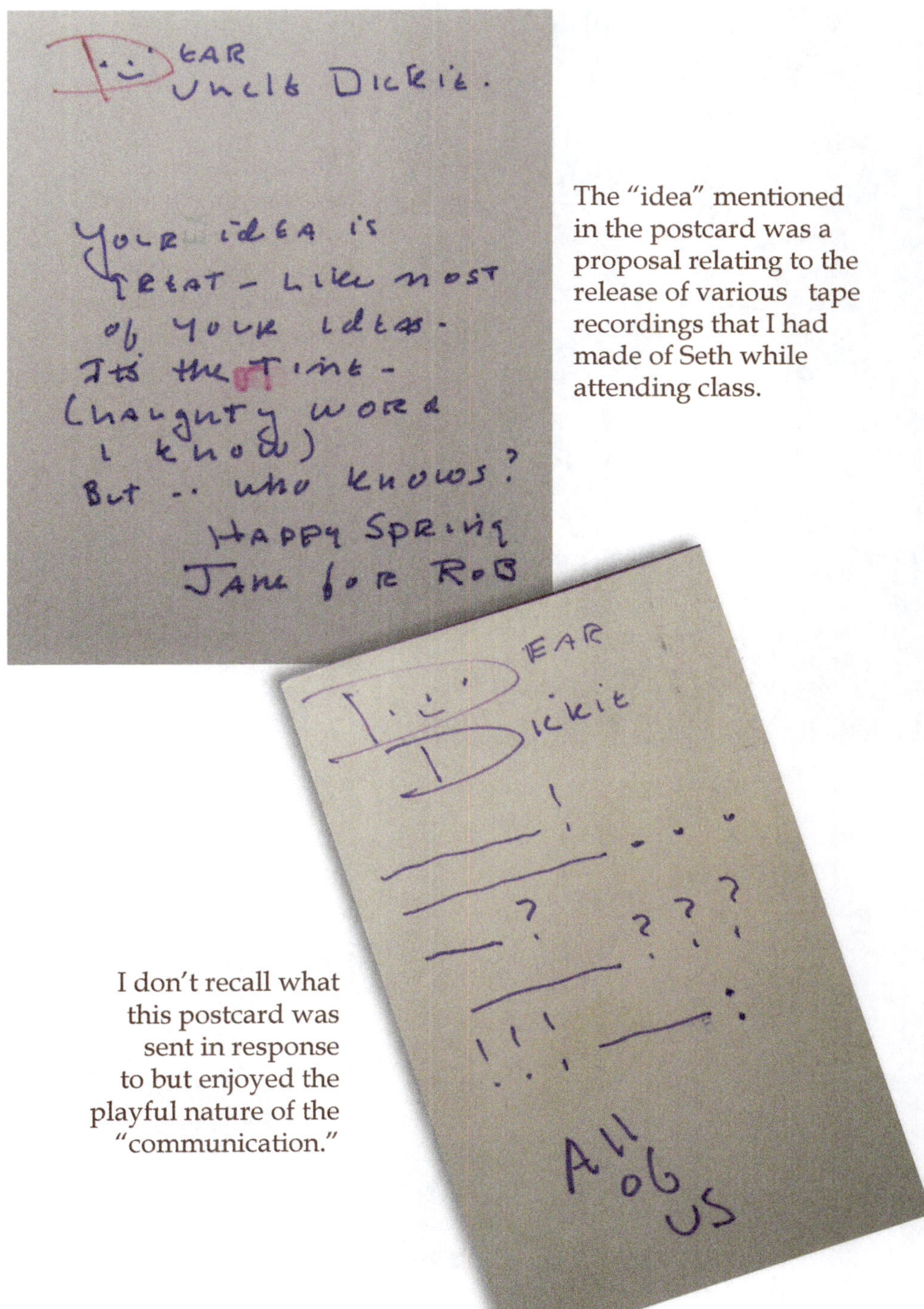

Dear Uncle Dickie.

Your idea is great – like most of your ideas.
It's the time –
(naughty word I know)
But .. who knows?
Happy Spring
Jane for Rob

The "idea" mentioned in the postcard was a proposal relating to the release of various tape recordings that I had made of Seth while attending class.

Dear Dickie

All of us

I don't recall what this postcard was sent in response to but enjoyed the playful nature of the "communication."

The drawing of the tree was done by Jane. Jane loved to paint and examples of her artwork appear as the covers on three of her books: *Adventures in Consciousness, The God of Jane, and Psychic Politics.* (The editions published by Moment Point Press.)

Dear Dickie.
The tree is the one outside our front window - sort of!
Your card is my favorite of all the ones we received and we wish you the best
Sumari 1980!
Love,
Rob. Jane & Co.

I had written Jane and Rob offering to put together a compilation containing recordings of Jane singing Sumari which I had taped over the years in class using my cassette recorder.

Wish I had a copy of "that poem" but like many other creative tidbits over the years things have a way of disappearing in time.

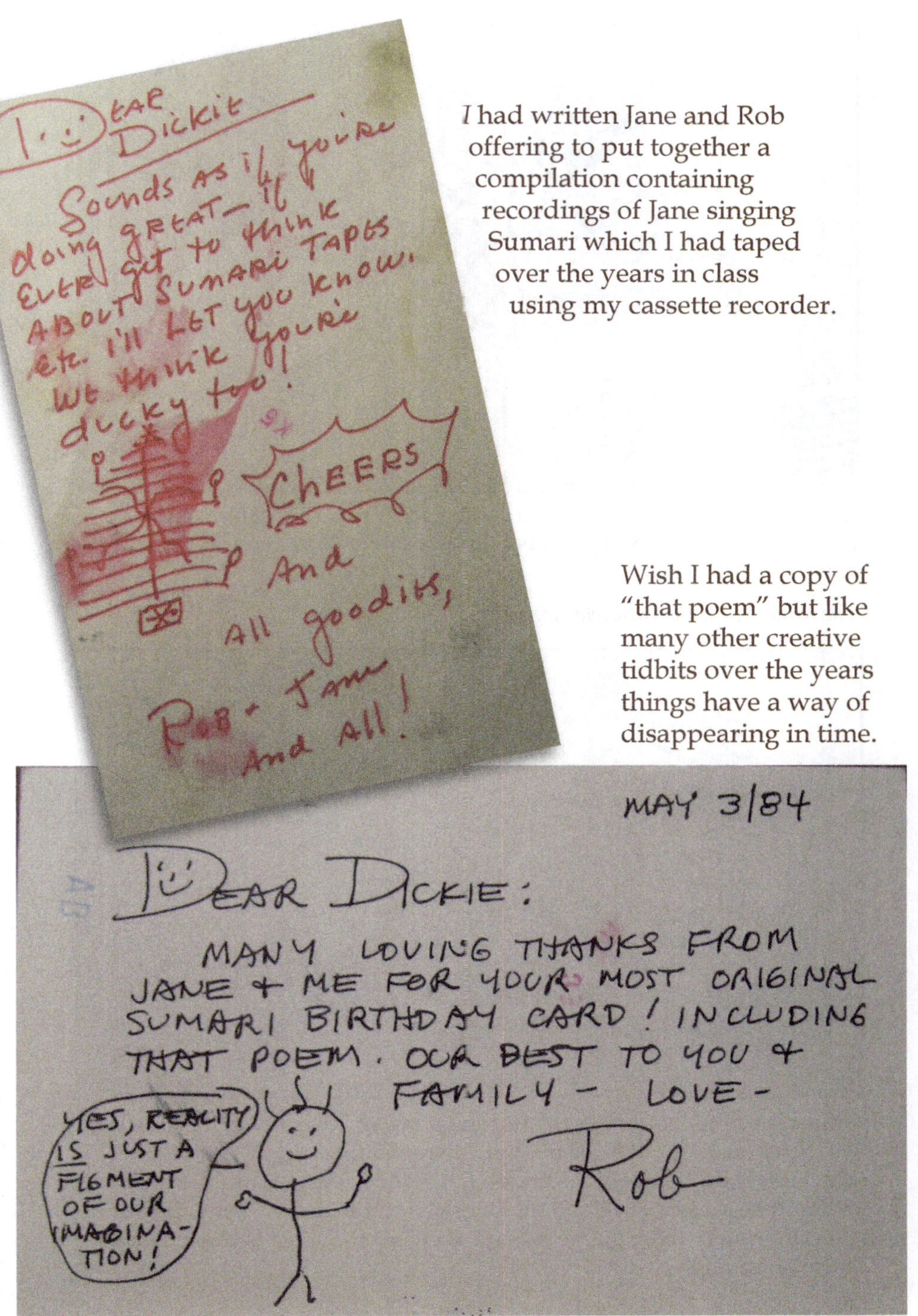

Dear Dickie

Sounds as if you're doing great — if ever get to think about Sumari tapes etc. I'll let you know. We think you're ducky too!

CHEERS

And All goodies,

Rob + Jane And All!

MAY 3/84

DEAR DICKIE:

MANY LOVING THANKS FROM JANE + ME FOR YOUR MOST ORIGINAL SUMARI BIRTHDAY CARD! INCLUDING THAT POEM. OUR BEST TO YOU + FAMILY - LOVE -

Rob

Regarding the words on the card, they seem to be evocative of the drawing, or the drawing seems to be evocative of the words. Either way, I love the card.

The drawing on the card was done by Rob.

Unlike the other cards which addressed me as "Dickie," in this one you see the name Richard Nissenbaum. Nissenbaum was my birth name which I legally changed to Kendall in 1990. My parents at the time were living in an area called Kendall, Florida, and the name "Kendall" had a certain ring to it for me, so when I decided to change my last name, I chose "Kendall."

The drawing on the card was done by Rob.

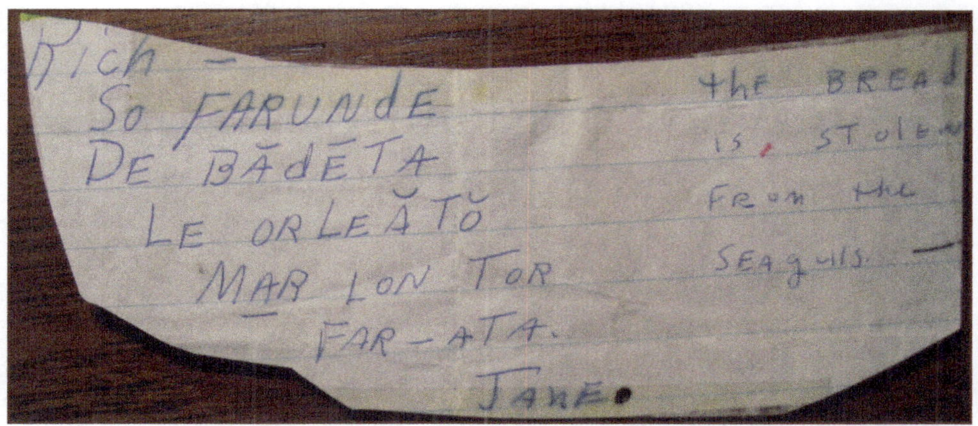

Rich —
So FARUNDE
DE BĂDETA
LE ORLEĂTŎ
MAR LON TOR
FAR-ATA.
Jane.

the BREAD
is STOLEN
FROM the
SEAGULLS —

See Chapter 13 from my book, *The Road To Elmira, Volume 1,* for an explanation of "The Bread is Stolen from the Seagulls."

The Sumari and the English translation were written by Jane on a scrap of paper which was scanned for inclusion in this book.

Jane seemed to enjoy celebrating Christmas, and I recall her once saying in class that if anyone had no place to go on Christmas Eve, they were welcome to come over to Jane and Rob's place.

The drawing on the card was done by Jane.

Interview of Richard Kendall by Winter Calvert

4-20-11

Winter: Today is April 20, 2011. My name is *Winter* Owen Calvert and I'm going to be interviewing Richard Kendall who was a long-time member of Jane Roberts' ESP Class; and a very popular student with Seth. So I am very honored to be able to talk to Rich today.

RK: Thank you very much. I am honored to speak with you.

Winter: I wanted to start with a little background, Rich. Just tell me a little bit like where you were born.

RK: I was born in Astoria, Queens, in New York City. When I was two years old my family moved to Bayside, Queens, a middle-class Jewish neighborhood, where I spent the next seventeen years of my life.

Winter: Tell me a little bit about your parents, your grandparents; are you the first generation?

RK: My grandparents were from Europe, and I wish I had taken the time to get more details about their lives. Every generation has a unique story to tell and it's a shame that we often don't take the time to record more fully what those before us have experienced. My grandparents were from Russia and Hungary, and while I don't know much about their lives before they came to America, I do know they left Europe to escape religious persecution of the Jews, and their Judaism remained a very important part of their lives here in America. My parents, to a lesser degree, felt that same sense of pride and identification with their Jewish heritage. But by the time it got to me, I was so far removed from the realities of World War II and the persecution of the Jews before then, that being Jewish just didn't have the same emotional relevance that it did for my grandparents or my parents.

Winter: Were your parents strict about it?

RK: When I was young they were strict in terms of following Jewish tradition, but as time went on they became more and more lax in regards to their adherence to Jewish customs. I think that's a very common thing that happened to a lot of families that grew up in my parents' generation.

Winter: Describe your childhood and some of the things you did.

RK: My childhood was fairly normal, though I'm not quite sure what normal is. We lived in a small apartment; in what they called garden apartments, in a housing complex called Clearview, which remains almost exactly the same as it was when I was growing up. These apartments were built after the war and were created with the idea of making housing affordable for the average working family. I don't know all the details but it was part of an overall government initiative to facilitate the growth of the middle class. I had a lot of friends while I was growing up for the area was densely populated with families that had all moved in about the same time.

Winter: So you played baseball or soccer?

RK: When I was young I loved sports. It was a big part of my life. And I identified with that aspect of myself, and got a lot of positive reinforcement from my athletic abilities. Sports were a very natural part of my being.

Winter: What was your favorite sport?

RK: I guess basketball. But the problem was that when I stopped growing I knew I wasn't tall enough to compete effectively at a professional level, so dreams of becoming a basketball star had to be abandoned.

Winter: Who were your heroes when you were a kid?

RK: Mainly sports figures. Basketball players or baseball players. Like most kids those were the figures we looked up to or that affected us the most.

Winter: Do you remember any funny incidents from your childhood; any trouble you got into.

RK: The mischief I got into as a young kid was pretty typical. Nothing in particular stands out for me along those lines. As I got older however, the "mischief" I became involved with became more serious, and I often marvel at the fact that I survived my teenage years relatively intact.

Winter: How did you do in school? Straight A?

RK: Wrong. My first few years in school, up through the third grade were fine. I did well and liked school. But there was a point, and it's hard to pinpoint exactly when, but there was a point around the fourth grade when I became very insecure about my intelligence and adopted the belief that I wasn't very smart. This affected my attitude toward school and negatively impacted my life in a lot of other areas as well. It took a long time for me to understand that this belief in my inferiority was simply that, *a belief,* and not necessarily a fact about reality. So from about the fourth grade on I had a very difficult time with school. In High School I missed so many classes that they threatened to not let me graduate, but with some serious pleading on my part, and the promise to make up for missed classes, thankfully I was allowed to graduate on time. I then went on to college— Staten Island Community College, (the only school I could get into in light of my grades). I was still living in Queens, New York, and to get to Staten Island required me to take a very long bus ride. Often I would take the bus to Staten Island and then instead of getting off and going to school, I would just sit there on the bus and let it take me back to Queens. I lasted about four months there and right about the time that finals were approaching at the end of my first semester, I decided to leave and hitchhike to California.

Winter: Tell me about some of your other beliefs as a child in terms of what you recall, or that you've thought about since.

RK: One of the beliefs I held very strongly as a child was the belief that youth was the pinnacle of our lives here on earth, and after that, all went steadily downhill. Seth once said the following to me during a class session in 1972 when I was twenty-two years old: *"If you believe that you will begin to deteriorate at 22 then so you shall."*

This belief in youth as being the high point of our life here on earth led me to have extremely strong resistances to the idea of becoming an adult. This in turn limited my progress and growth in many different ways. I associated becoming an adult with losing all the magic and fun of life; again a belief, as opposed to a fact of existence. Perhaps part of me acquired that belief as a result of looking at my father and the way he was living his life. My father was a good man, worked a lot of hours to support his family, but I don't think he enjoyed his life very much during the years I was growing up. He would often come home after work feeling totally exhausted, would go to his room, close the door, and disappear for the night. I was speaking in class one evening about how I felt that I had lost all the magic and fun of my youth and didn't know if I would ever recapture it. Seth then looked at me and said, *"We will see that you do, so that you will see that there are many ways to break an egg, and also so that you will not have to look back for the rest of your life with envy toward the ecstasies of your youth."*

Winter: Tell me a little bit about your relationship with your parents.

RK: Bad.

Winter: As a child or even as an adult?

RK: Things turned bad at an early age. As we look back on our lives, (if we do look back on our lives) we can make connections and comprehend things that earlier on, when we were in the midst of living them, we did not get at all. For example, while I found myself with great anger toward my parents much of the time, in looking back today I can feel some sympathy for them, realizing the difficulties they faced in dealing with a very rebellious and stubborn young man; that being me of course. And who knows what issues they were dealing with in their lives apart from me. But my parents' attempts to discipline me over the years were often met with great resistance on my part, even if their actions were motivated by a genuine concern for me, which I don't think was always the case. Authority figures of any kind really pushed my buttons and still do to some extent. So there was a real battle of wills that went on between me and my mother in particular, and when that happens the possibilities for understanding go out the window, and nobody wins.

Winter: Was your mother the nurturing type and your father the disciplinarian or how do you remember that?

RK: My father at some point just kind of tuned out. No doubt there were reasons for this and I wish it was possible to go back and ask him what was going on in his life at the time. Maybe it was financial pressures, or aspirations he had that weren't fulfilled, but as a child you're not about to say, "Dad, what's motivating you to act in such and such a way. I remember an incident that occurred when I was about nine years old. I was taking a shower and thinking about how other kid's dads often took them places on the weekend and did things with them, and how my father never did that with me. And I just spontaneously started sobbing in the shower and my mother heard me; and when I got out she asked me what was going on. I told her why I was so upset and the next weekend my father took me to some park for the afternoon, but after that, things went back to the way they had been. So while my father continued to do the mandatory things that a parent does in terms of providing for a family, emotionally he became absent. I think as a result of his unwillingness or inability to deal with the emotional realities of his children, an extra burden fell upon my mother to do so. Being high strung, this was difficult for her, and subsequently difficult for me. It's too bad that earlier in our lives when things like this are happening, we're not able to pause and have a dialogue with those around us to discover what is really going on. But I guess that's a lot to ask from a kid. I do think if one were to acquaint themselves with the Seth material from a very early age, and try to utilize many of the ideas, the discourse between parents and children (not to mention the discourse with everyone else) would take on a whole different tenor, and issues that otherwise would remain hidden could be brought out into the open and dealt with far more effectively.

Winter: You had brothers and sisters?

RK: I have an older brother who lives in Maryland. He's about six years older than me and as a result of that time difference his life was not surrounded by the same influences that were present in my life. Drugs, Woodstock, and the whole Hippie movement were not part of his reality. My brother, unlike me, did very well in school, and was pretty straight-laced compared to me at the time. I also have a sister who is two years older than me, and she also did very well in school, and rarely got into trouble. So it must have been a bit shocking for my parents when a third one comes along who is so different from what they had experienced with their first two children. The contrasts in families are often very interesting to observe.

Winter: Were you close to your brother and sister?

RK: Not particularly. But I was very close to my friends. There was this very strong bond that existed between us for many years. Many of the friends that I made while growing up ended up going to Seth class with me, so we shared some important experiences together.

Winter: Who were those, do you remember all the names?

RK: Jeffrey Marcus, Lawrence Davidson, Richard Wolinsky, Barrie Gellis, Alan Bornstein, Rick Stack; they were some of the first ones to go to Seth class and who continued to go for many years.

Winter: Do you all still talk occasionally?

RK: We talk but not nearly as much as we did when we were all hanging out together in our teens and in our twenties. As with any group of friends we went our separate ways though some of us remained close through the years.

Winter: Tell me about Woodstock.

RK: Woodstock, in my estimation, reflected a deeply felt dissatisfaction among many young people with the way the world was operating. It represented a rejection of traditional religious and societal values. At the same time there were many who still deeply believed in those values, so there was a significant split in the mass consciousness of this country that in its own way continues today. The status quo on many levels was being challenged, and Woodstock was symbolic of a strong desire within many of my generation to forge a new direction for ourselves, for this country, and ultimately for the world. Many of us just weren't drawn to the life-models that had been in place for many decades. The prospect of going out to make a lot of money, attending church or synagogue once a week, getting married, having children, and planning for retirement so one could sit around drinking scotch and soda at the country club just wasn't very inspiring. In short, repeating the same life patterns that our parents pursued was not something we wished to do. And while the generation of the sixties did not make the world over into a mecca of peace and love as they had hoped, I think Woodstock was evidence that individual and mass consciousness was changing. I also think it's no accident that the Seth material started becoming quite popular in the late sixties, during the same time period that Woodstock occurred.

Winter: Were you into the music at the time. Was that a big part of it?

RK: It was a tremendously creative time, and subjects that had been taboo in terms of public discussion were now being addressed openly in all of the arts, and appearing on the world stage in a variety of milieus. It wasn't just that the envelope was being pushed to new limits, but new envelopes were being created. I think the whole technological revolution represents a further evolution of consciousness as each generation seeks to expand the seeming boundaries of the psyche that characterized the generation before them. I can only wonder what the next generation will bring in terms of creative expansion and technological innovation.

Winter: Who did you go to Woodstock with? Did you go by yourself?

RK: I did not go by myself but I couldn't tell you who I went with, and I couldn't tell you for the obvious reasons – I was probably pretty stoned. I was taking a lot of drugs at the time as were a lot of people in my generation. It was one of the avenues we all thought might lead to answers, and it also served to alleviate the inner pain and confusion that a large number of us felt as we were trying to find a place for ourselves in a world that often seemed quite mad. But ultimately, we discovered that drugs didn't supply us with the answers we sought, and sadly, the misuse of drugs led to many lives being destroyed at a very young age. When I think about friends that died from drug overdoses it is indeed sad. I don't take drugs anymore and haven't done so for over thirty years. It doesn't have to do with moral reasons, but I don't want to impair my mental or physical health in any way, and drugs often lead to such impairment. As long as we're on the subject, while I don't smoke marijuana, I think marijuana is a natural product of the earth and taken in moderation I don't see any reason to prohibit its use.

Winter: Did you have any good experiences with drugs?

RK: That question is very broad and to adequately answer it would require more space and time than is available in this interview. While certain drugs did expand my consciousness in some ways, it happened at a price. There are downsides to using drugs in an attempt to alter one's consciousness, and that downside doesn't exist if we utilize the natural mechanisms that are already in place within our consciousness; mechanisms that don't require any kind of outside or artificial stimulation. The whole concept of how we use drugs as a society, whether for medical purposes or for purposes of consciousness expansion is a subject that I believe is worthy of greater study.

Winter: Do you think there is some kind of connection between the first landing on the moon and Woodstock, which occurred within a month of each other?

RK: That's an interesting question, and it's funny you bring it up because in my book, *The Road To Elmira,* I mention that very thing. I believe both events, Woodstock and the landing on the moon, represented an inner movement within mass consciousness to go beyond previously accepted boundaries, and that both events in their own way sent out ripples to shake up our ideas of what was possible both on an individual and on a mass basis. And again, I don't believe the timing of those events (or any events for that matter) are accidental.

Winter: Did you register for the draft?

RK: During the time when I was eligible for the draft they had a lottery system, and that was one lottery you didn't want to win. The way it worked was that you were assigned a number, and if your number was picked you were required by law to go to your local draft board to undergo a pre-induction physical. At that time the Vietnam War was raging, so being called in to your local draft board with the possibility of being shipped off to Vietnam was no joking matter. In the book, *Conversations With Seth,* by Susan M. Watkins, she speaks about the draft and recounts a story by Jeff Marcus of what he did when called down for his pre-induction physical and was faced with the possibility of "serving his country" by participating in the Vietnam War. I think it's worth reading.

Winter: So tell me a little bit about how you got introduced to Jane Roberts' classes.

RK: When the 1960's ended it was obvious to me that I couldn't turn to religion or to drugs, or to any of the current systems in place to bring me any satisfying answers about life, and death, and whatever might exist in between. So I started delving into the writings of various metaphysical authors. To name but a few, I studied the works of Carl Jung, Joseph Campbell, Gerald Massey, Alvin Boyd Kuhn; Madame Blavatsky, George Ivanovich Gurdjieff, and many others, as each of them addressed the greater issues of life from their own perspective. Then a friend of mine mentioned to me that he ran across this fellow named Francois who was teaching metaphysical courses from his apartment in New York City, and suggested this might be worth looking into. Francois was teaching a philosophy called "Gnosticism," which had been practiced by various Christian sects in the early centuries. And while there were certain elements in his teachings that were similar to those followed by the Gnostics, Francois had his own very personal take on how this universe worked, and was not shy in sharing it. The idea of meeting a live person (as opposed to reading some dead author) who might be able to shed light upon some of the questions that had been plaguing me since I was a young boy, was a very exciting prospect. So plans were set in motion to meet this Francois person, which was the beginning of a journey that ultimately led me to Jane Roberts' living room and to Seth.

Winter: But you didn't see Francois as another authority figure?

RK: Good question! I think one of the reasons I didn't see him as an authority figure was because he didn't fit the traditional image. He had an exotic air about him; the way he spoke, the way he dressed, his whole demeanor didn't fit in with the usual image that authority figures held for me. I started to take in whatever he was teaching without questioning any of it, which was a real shift for me, to suddenly not question someone that actually I should have been questioning at every turn.

Winter: And Seth talked about him a little bit.

RK: Yes, Seth did talk about him. What I didn't know at the time that I was studying under Francois was that he had contacted Jane Roberts on numerous occasions and wanted to meet with her. But in Jane's words, Francois used to drive her up a wall. He liked to think of himself as a kindred spirit with Jane but she didn't feel that way at all about him. All of this I found out later on. Jane felt that his brand of esoteric philosophy was completely opposite to what she and Seth were teaching. Francois believed there was this secret knowledge and that if one wasn't properly prepared to receive it, this knowledge could prove to be very dangerous. Seth and Jane on the other hand were putting forth exactly the opposite message; that this knowledge was free and available to anyone who sought it, that it was our birthright, and there were no dangers connected to looking within, exploring our dreams, or delving into any aspects of our consciousness.

Winter: Do you remember how you got introduced to the first class.

RK: Sure. What happened was, well just to back up a bit with Francois, his intention was to open up a school whose ultimate purpose would be to teach "the unconscious masses" about the true nature of reality. And to this end he would first be teaching a select group of followers the occult secrets he was supposedly privy to, and his followers would then serve as his instruments in the world to educate the masses. It's an old theme in different clothing. As part of his teaching we were given a list of books we had to study and read in a specific order as dictated by Francois. But one of the students came across the book, *The Seth Material*, which was not on Francois' list at the time She started telling the other students about this book and I decided to check it out. From the first few pages it struck a definite chord in me. I felt as if I was returning to something I had once been in touch with but left behind a long time ago. As I read about Jane and her classes I of course wanted to go to one of them. I asked Francois if that would be okay, for I didn't do much without his approval at that time. While he gave me the okay, he also made a point of stressing the fact that Jane was not very evolved spiritually, but that Seth was more in line with the level of enlightenment that Francois claimed to have achieved. So I wrote Jane a letter and asked about the possibility of visiting her or going to one of her classes. I signed the letter "Your respectful initiate," which today makes me cringe a bit, as I imagine what Jane's reaction must have been to that closing remark. But Jane did write me back and said that if I was ever up in the Elmira area to give her a call and she would let me stop by. I was delighted by her response, but wasn't all that anxious to follow up at that time because I was still immersed in following Francois and studying his teachings. But then one afternoon in December of 1971 I received a phone call informing me that Francois had dropped dead on the street in *New York City*, and with that, everything changed.

Francois was relatively young by the way, only in his forties, and had seemed to be quite healthy. No one knew for sure the cause of his death, but what I did know was that after devoting two years of my life to following him and studying his philosophy I was now guru-less. I started to feel a little desperate because I had become so used to relying on Francois that when he died I felt like I needed to replace him as soon as possible. And that's when I thought of Jane and Seth and the letter I had written to Jane some months earlier. So I wrote her another letter asking again about going to a class, but in the interim my friend Jeffrey decided to call her. She told Jeff that if we wanted to come up to class we could.

And so Francois died in December of 1971, and on January 4th, 1972 we went to our first Seth class.

Winter: Who was in the car?

RK: It was me, Jeff Marcus, and Rick Stack. Jane and her husband Rob were renting two apartments on the second floor of an old Victorian house in Elmira, New York, and as I walked up the stairs Jane happened to have been in the hallway. She said hello, and then asked me my name. I said Richard, and she paused for a moment as if something clicked inside her head. She said, Are you sure that's what you are called? I looked at her and said, yes, my name is Richard. But in truth, nobody ever called me Richard. My nickname was Dickie and everybody called me Dickie. I should have known right then and there that I was in for a lot more than I had consciously bargained for.

RK: Winter: So you went to that first class in January of 1972 and what was your impression?

RK: I had a number of impressions. Class used to have what they called reincarnational dramas, which of course was completely new to me. These "dramas" weren't anything that were planned beforehand, but would spontaneously arise, where people would find themselves *reliving* (for lack of a better word) memories or events from other lives. And often this would occur between various members of the class on any given evening. There was a fellow in class that night named Fred. I had never met Fred before, yet every time Fred spoke I felt intense anger toward him. I was wondering where all this anger was coming from when all of a sudden one of the women in class looked at me and said, Why are you feeling all this anger toward Fred? I immediately went into defensive mode denying that I was feeling any anger toward Fred. This same woman then said to me, Why is Fred on trial? Jane then went into trance and started singing Sumari, which is a trance language she would sing at various times in class. It is not a specific language that was spoken during any historical period, but I found out later that one of the purposes of Sumari was to jog within us memories of past lives. So Jane started singing in Sumari, and then motioned for me and Fred to come up and stand on either side of her chair. And as she continued singing this Sumari song she took Fred's hands and my hands and clasped them together. So Fred and I were listening to this Sumari song and staring at each other and at one point I smiled at Fred as if to say, Okay, I'm not angry at you anymore, *though I knew I was still feeling some anger toward him*. Right at that moment, Jane, while still in trance, vigorously shook our hands. When she did that I laughed, and then I really did let the anger go. Jane then came out of the Sumari trance and before the blink of an eye Seth came through, looked at me, and said *"Let that be a lesson to you."* I then sat back down near the bay windows in the back of the room trying to make some sense out of what had just happened.

Jane and some of the other members of class started commenting about images they were receiving while the Sumari were singing; images of me being a judge and Fred being on trial for committing some sexual act that was considered immoral at the time. And I had meted out a very severe sentence to him which relegated him to the role of outcast in society, and they were all picking up these similar images and impressions.

On the way home that night, Jeffrey told me how amazed he was when I started singing along with the Sumari when I was standing by Jane's chair. Now it was my turn to be amazed because I truly had no recollection of doing that. So all in all enough had happened during that first class to lead me to want to come back, and come back I did for many years

Winter: So you started going once a week?

RK: Yes. It was about a five hour drive each way and we would drive up once a week on Tuesdays. We'd leave about one o'clock in the afternoon so as to give ourselves time for a lunch break along the way. Class would begin around seven in the evening and end around eleven, eleven thirty. Then we'd drive back that same night. It was about two hundred forty miles each way, but the distance didn't really bother us because there was a lot of anticipation as we wondered each week what class might hold in store for us. Unlike school for example, where you might receive an assignment to read chapters five through ten, summarize them, and then come back the following week with the results, in Jane's class we were writing the chapters as we went along, and that included Jane as well.

Winter: Did you take notes in the class?

RK: I didn't take notes in the class, but when I got home I would write down events and feelings from that night's class that stood out for me. As I was doing this it was not done with the intention, at least not consciously, of one day writing a book about these experiences, but I was just doing it for my own personal record.

Winter: Sometimes someone would take notes and type them up and then bring them back.

RK: Seth made a point that he wouldn't come through unless there was someone in class who would record the sessions. So there was always someone who would tape record the classes using one of those old cassette recorders, and then either that same person or someone else would create a transcript of the session.

Winter: Did you ever go more than once a week?

RK: Not often, but every now and then I would go up to Elmira and stay for a few days before class instead of driving up and returning home that same night. My friend Barrie Gellis (who now runs an online Seth site) had moved to Elmira, so sometimes I would go up to visit him on nights other than when classes were held. Also, Jane and Rob would have these get-togethers at their apartment on Friday nights, and occasionally I would attend those as well. They were not Seth classes, and some of the people there had not been to any of Jane's classes, but were friends of Jane and Rob from the area. But Jane was Jane, and while she could engage in small talk, Jane's mind was like a finely tuned antenna functioning on many different levels at once; always looking for the hidden meanings in what others might view as simply the mundane events of the moment.

Winter: Did the New York boys expand, did the group expand?

RK: What happened was that Jeffrey, more than anyone else, made a point of trying to bring as many different people to Seth class as possible. He had a van at the time, so he was able to bring up lots of new people over the years. He would always have to check with Jane first, and for some reason she was always a bit reluctant, yet she'd eventually give in and allow it. I remember one week Jeffrey was asking her about bringing some new people to class and Jane started saying how we have so many people in class already, etc. but then finally agreed. And I looked at her and for some reason I made the sarcastic comment: "She's just a girl who can't say no." And she shot me a look that could kill. I don't know why that came out of my mouth, but her buttons could be pushed just like anyone else's. One last point about Jeffrey and the car rides to class. Before he had the van, he had a regular four-door sedan and at times he would ride in the trunk so as to make room for someone else who otherwise would not have been able to come up due to a lack of space in the car. He didn't mind doing this, did so voluntarily, and furthermore, he liked to have the trunk completely closed while someone else would be driving his car. Then on the way back from class we'd pull into some small town at 3:00 in the morning to get gas and out would pop Jeffrey from the trunk, stopping the gas station attendant in his tracks. At least it probably gave the guy working at the gas station something to talk about when asked by a friend the next day how work went.

Winter: So you got along with Jane?

RK: I loved Jane, and got along with her really well. And I know she was very fond of all the guys from New York. When we first started going to class the atmosphere in that room was pretty laid back, despite the unique nature of what was happening. And then we rambled in with our long hair and rebellious and boisterous nature, and I think it would be fair to say we injected a lot of life into that class. Jane once made a comment to the effect that she identified with us guys a lot more than she did with some of the other people in class, and I think she did so because in her own way she had that same kind of rambunctious and rebellious energy. One thing I'll add that I learned early on was that if you ever tried to push Jane too much or pressure her, she did not respond well. People who wanted too much attention from Jane or were constantly seeking her approval didn't fare very well. But if you just let her do her thing, in time you would get whatever you needed. But she did not like being pushed.

Winter: What was Jane's attitude about drugs?

RK: That's another interesting question. An incident occurred in 1979 during one of the last classes any of us attended. Most of us were hardly ever taking drugs anymore but this one night one of the guys from New York had gone up and had taken some pills to get high, and one of the pills had fallen on the floor, and Jane found it after we had left. None of us knew this at the time. A couple of weeks later I was coming up to Elmira with a few friends, (also former class members) to help a woman I knew move. She was moving from the Elmira area to New York City. I called Jane and asked if we could stop by, and to my great surprise she said no, and was quite adamant about it. Jane's response was not typical at all of the way she would normally respond to us so I knew something was wrong, though I didn't know what it was. One of my friends was so upset at her refusal to see us that she called Jane back and was crying on the phone. Jane then told her how she had found a pill on the floor during that last class and said that it was very disappointing to her. She said that after all these years of attending classes, and with everything she was trying to teach us about the nature of consciousness, the fact that some of us still felt it necessary to take drugs to feel the magic of our being or make a connection with the universe was very disheartening. Jane wondered aloud if she had done a very good job of teaching us. Finally, she did let us come over and we had a nice visit. I remember other times when Jane wondered whether the books she was writing and the classes she had taught were really helping anyone, and whether the material was really getting through to people. She wasn't looking for praise or approval when she asked these questions, but she genuinely had her doubts as to whether the work she was doing was really making a positive difference in people's lives.

Winter: Were there particular sessions or comments that Seth made to you that meant the most to you.

RK: There were many comments Seth made that affected me strongly, but the following comes to mind. I was in my early twenties and was feeling extremely frustrated with my life. I felt adrift and just didn't know what direction to move in. On the way up to class that day I was thinking, I'm going to ask Seth for help tonight. And then I said, no, (the conversation you have in your own mind) as I told myself I had to stop looking to Seth and Jane for all my answers and had to start looking to myself. So I went up to class that evening and I didn't say a word about how frustrated I was feeling. And during the middle of that class Seth looked at me and said the following: *I have a word for you tonight, when you did not ask for my advice. Now, play paddle ball with the universe. Play paddle ball with the universe! In more mundane terms, in much more mundane terms, get out! Go into the world! Seek your own sustenance.* He went on to address other issues that were concerning me and his words were right on point.

Winter: Did Seth ever give you your entity name?

RK: Yes, and I never liked it very much.

Winter: What is it?

RK: Ringdano.

Winter: Does it have any meaning or feeling to you?

RK: It doesn't really do much for me. Now Sumari was a different story. He gave some of us individual Sumari songs which Jane sang to us one evening. The Sumari song I got did resonate with me and I have a copy of it on tape and listen to it from time to time. The idea behind an individual Sumari song was that you were supposed to memorize the song, and then during times of difficulty, or at any time you might feel like it, sing the song to yourself, and doing this was supposed to help harmonize various portions of your being. So the Sumari thing I definitely connected with, but Ringdano just never brought up any particular feelings within me.

Winter: I never heard that name. The name doesn't have a meaning? Did you ever try to look it up?

RK: I did google it at one point but didn't find anything relevant. Some of the entity names Seth gave out were very common names so I never really got what the whole entity name thing was all about. Seth overall wasn't big on giving labels to things but he also gave various names to what he called families of consciousness. Seth said there were different families of consciousness and went on to name them as well as to explain the various traits that characterized each family of consciousness. Sumari was the name of one of those families and was the family that I was supposed to belong to.

Winter: Did you ever question it? Did you ever say, I'm not sure if this is all true? I'm not sure if I'm doing the right thing?

RK: I questioned it numerous times, and still have my questions. But I don't look at the Seth material anymore in terms of true and false or black and white. Enough has happened in my life, both my inner life and my outer life, that I know there is an overall validity to the material. That doesn't mean I can swear that every statement Seth ever made is the absolute gospel, but I don't need to believe that to continue to devote my time and energy to exploring this incredible body of work. Jane herself, to the surprise of many people, would also question the material, and never stopped trying to understand who or what Seth was. And Seth himself acknowledged there was bound to be some distortions in the material due to the limitations of words and the fact that Jane's own prejudices might color some of the material she was receiving. But the material was not designed to become a new dogma to be quoted chapter and verse, a point specifically addressed by Seth as well as by Jane.

As I view it, the Seth material is a roadmap to the inner dimensions of our being, and while points of correspondence will of course exist, the Seth material as far as I am concerned is the Seth material according to Richard, or Lawrence, or Robert, or whoever is reading it, and will be interpreted through our individual perspectives as well it should be. To speak in terms of being an expert on the Seth material to me is a misnomer; but if one must think in terms of experts, I think the only real expert on the Seth material is Seth.

I just don't think there is one objective reality that exists in the exact same terms for all of us, yet at the same time I am not saying that there is not truth. But we each must find our own truths and because we are all unique they will of necessity not be the truths that others may discover. At the same time I believe there are "places" within us where mass consciousness convenes, and from those places we create common realities that transcend any individual differences. And it is from those interior meeting spots that I believe mass consciousness can work great changes upon the outer world, changes that will benefit all of us.

Winter: What about dreams, did you ever get into dream work?

RK: I have always had a relatively easy time remembering my dreams but must admit that over recent years I have not been very rigorous in terms of writing them down. At other points in my life I was more disciplined and recorded my dreams on a daily basis and would also try to interpret them. Seth and Jane emphasized the importance of dreams over and over again and encouraged us to try to remember them, to write them down, and to think about their meaning. I think dreams serve many purposes and intersect with daily reality in ways we have yet to understand. Seth also told us that dreams contain solutions to many problems both on an individual as well as a mass basis. He told us we should suggest on any given night before going to sleep that we would have a dream that would provide answers to a specific problem we might be grappling with, and then in the morning to write down whatever we remember, and think about what the dream might be trying to tell us.

I know there are some people who are doing fantastic work with their dreams and have become adept at lucid dreaming, where they become fully aware and conscious while in the dreamstate. My friend Emmy van Swaaij in the Netherlands is one of those folks and I'm constantly amazed at the things she discovers in working with her dreams.

Winter: What are you working on now in your life in terms of personal growth. I'm not sure that's a fair question.

RK: That's definitely a fair question and the answer, to be equally fair, is that in certain terms I'm working on the same issues that have challenged me my entire life. I think we come into this life with certain blueprints containing issues we have chosen ahead of time to explore. I'm not saying that free will doesn't operate, for the blueprints we choose are chosen freely, and can be altered at any time. But I think there are various issues consciousness chooses to deal with ahead of time so to speak, and exploring those issues is a lifelong endeavor.

Seth often used to tell us that instead of thinking of problems in the way we usually do, to instead try to see them as challenges, which puts an entirely different spin on how we view the issues we face in our daily lives. The official line of consciousness says you have a problem and you solve it and that's the end of the story. That may work with mathematics or science or in business, but I don't think that applies to the nature of consciousness, or how our lives operate. And to me that's not a negative, because it doesn't mean you do not progress or improve the quality of your life in a given area. But if you can view a problem in a more expansive way, as a challenge for example, then the solutions you come up with will also be more expansive.

Winter: What do you like to do with your free time?

RK: I play guitar (not very well) and like to compose songs as well as listen to music. I'm also a big fan of movies. I love movies. There's a book people may be familiar with by Jane Roberts called *The Education of Oversoul Seven*, which I always thought would make a wonderful movie. On and off I've been in touch with the fellow who owns the movie rights to that book and that's a project I would love to be involved with should the opportunity arise one day.

Winter: Where would you like to be in five years? What would you like to be doing?

RK: When I was in my early twenties if someone would have asked me that question I would have said something along the lines of wanting to be fantastically wealthy, famous, maybe the head of a movie studio, and living in a huge mansion off the coast of California overlooking the Pacific ocean. And although there is nothing wrong with any of those things, my aspirations have changed as I have gotten older. Waking up in a modest home next to someone I love and earning a living from creative endeavors that bring me satisfaction will be more than enough for me.

Winter: Is there anything that you still would like to do before you pass away?

RK: Yes. I'd like to go to Disneyland. Just kidding. Actually, I've been there and it's pretty cool. But to answer your question, I'd like to make a list of all the places that Marguerite de Valois visited and lived in during her lifetime. I'd then put them in chronological order, and following that order I'd go to France and revisit them. I'd take pictures of each place, jot down any impressions that came to mind, and put it all in a little book which I'd hide away in some dusty attic somewhere. Then one day many years after I passed away someone would discover this book, and would wonder what kind of odd fellow would write such an odd little book.

Winter: What would you like to say to students of the future. Imagine somebody is reading this a hundred, or two hundred years from now. What do you want to say to them?

RK: It's ironic in certain terms because here I went to class all those years, studying with Seth and Jane, and yet I think the biggest lesson from all of it is to look to ourselves for answers; to trust (in the words of Seth) the authority of our own psyches. We grow up being taught to look to others for answers, to look outside of ourselves, to not trust that little voice that speaks to us in the day as well as in the night. Yet that voice springs from those inner dimensions where the true journeys of consciousness take place, and where the greatest discoveries will be made. And while I speak of looking within, this is not meant to demean or denigrate the value of our physical lives or the world we currently reside in. For the work we do within is meant to transform the world without, so that the physical world in which we presently dwell can shine more brightly, not only for ourselves, but for everyone on our planet. I believe that as we lift ourselves up we automatically help lift up the entire race of which we are part.

Leading us back to ourselves is one of the prime directives that underlie the Seth material. And getting us to look to other aspects within ourselves for answers, without our outer ego feeling threatened was a challenge that Jane and Seth carried off brilliantly. For they knew a part of us was going to fight like hell to hold on to old ideas and old habits of consciousness, to maintain a psychological status quo, so they had to be smart about the way they pulled the rug out from under us, and smart they were.

Winter: Do you have any favorite Seth quotes that you think about from time to time?

RK: Yes. *"If it stops being fun, stop doing it."* Another Seth quote that comes to mind that I particularly like is the following: *"Flesh and blood has miraculous dimensions. Perfection is not one of them."*

Winter: is there anything else you'd like to add?

RK: Only to reiterate that the more you rely on things or people outside of yourself for answers, the greater the distance will become between yourself and the magic of your own being.

Winter: Thanks for talking with us today.

RK: Thank you.

CPSIA information can be obtained at www.ICGtesting.com
Printed in the USA
BVOW11s2110200214

345575BV00007B/19/P

9 780983 577645